KISS THE SON

JOSEPHINE C. SHARIF

Copyright © 2010 by Josephine C. Sharif

Kiss The Son
by Josephine C. Sharif

Printed in the United States of America

ISBN 9781612153544

All rights reserved solely by the author. The author guarantees all contents are original and do not infringe upon the legal rights of any other person or work. No part of this book may be reproduced in any form without the permission of the author. The views expressed in this book are not necessarily those of the publisher.

Unless otherwise indicated, Bible quotations are taken from The Holy Bible, King James Version.

Cover design and original cover art entitled "Caught Up" by Josephine C. Sharif.

www.xulonpress.com

my first fruit novel

KISS THE SON

Dedicated to my Lord and Savior Jesus Christ

"Behold, for peace I had great bitterness:
but thou hast in love to my soul delivered it from
the pit of corruption:
for thou hast cast all my sins behind thy back."
—Isaiah 38:17

You are truly the Lover of my soul
I give You all the glory!

Acknowledgments

Without Jesus, I can do nothing—but I can do all things through Christ who strengthens me! I wish to acknowledge my husband Fard Sharif who inspired me to love and worship God. Thank you for supporting my lifelong Jesus addiction! I bless all my sons and daughters, Cornell, Najla, Yasin, Ayesha and Jabriel and granddaughter Niomi—you all kept me motivated and grounded in our "eight is enough" family during this season in my life following my mother's death. In memory of my late mother Grace and our church hopping experiences that led me to my current church home, I bless you and may you rest in peace in the arms of our Savior. Thank you for the family style inspiration to my sisters Robin, Tiffany, Juana, Cecilia and brothers Michael, Joey, Harold, and yes another Michael and my Daddy Joe who keeps me smiling! Bless my mother-in-law Zahirah Mama Rosie and father-in-law Ahmad who have been sweet and supportive to us—thanks for keeping watch. Bless my cousin Delora and spiritual law counselor Zina—you are both prophetesses from the Lord! God bless my pastor and his wife, Apostle H. Daniel Wilson and Pastor Beverly Wilson and the entire church family of Valley Kingdom Ministries International where I have become rooted in Christ Jesus. Shout out to Rhema Word Ministry and all my fellow Sunday School Teachers! Bless those caring Christian Attorneys Cathe Evans Williams and

Deadra Woods Stokes who over the past ten years have helped me grow spiritually in the workplace.

**IT TAKES A VILLAGE TO RAISE ME!
I LOVE YOU ALL! BE BLESSED!**

KISS THE SON

"Kiss the Son, lest He be angry, and ye perish from the way, when His wrath is kindled but a little. Blessed are all they that put their trust in Him."
—**Psalm 2:12 (KJV)**

X's & O's. To seal wedding vows, to openly show love, to prove solidarity, oneness—a kiss is all those things and means so much. To our Precious Bridegroom Jesus Christ, it is a sweet sign of worship to blow Him a love kiss. He first loved us with a kiss, an *X* turned on its side became a cross. There Jesus proved His love to His Bride, the Church. On the cross, the *X*, the kiss, changed forever an estranged and heartbroken world. Now, it is an open invitation—*Kiss the Son*—with a promise of eternal life and blessings in Jesus' Holy Name.

Prelude To A Kiss

The Wedding Party
Five Years Earlier

SHENIR SANCHEZ. Lord Jesus I love you because you heard my prayers and answered them all. I will forever be grateful to you! Shane Houghton and I were the New Millennium Lovers, like stars in a dream wedding held June 2, 2000, outdoors in the lovely rose garden in the backyard of my parents' Chicago home. Ever so handsome in his white tux complementing his caramel brown complexion, Shane walked center isle down the flower-lined path toward the front of the garden. His best man Dirksen was just a few steps behind him paired up with Vanessa, my best friend and maid of honor. Moments later, my little sister Mimi at age 16 only five years younger than me, walked down the isle paired up with her friend Carlos. A few maids later, the little Shirley-temple-curled flower girl, Reissa, Shane's five-year-old cousin, scattered white rose petals along a red carpeted pathway. And finally, my grand entrance in a lovely white silk and lace gown with pearl beading around the neck just like I've always wished for—perfect, just perfect. Shane's hazel eyes lit up as he smiled at me approvingly. All our guests were a multi-cultural blend of family and friends, with my half African American and half Spanish relatives mixing and mingling with Shane's South Side Chicago Black Baptist clan. My father Christo Sanchez was not there to treasure this moment of my life, having lost his battle with heart disease a year ago. Lord, I wept with all my heart that Daddy couldn't give me away. It hurt me so much when he passed away, but he told me to be strong for him and Mamasita. So, with your help, Lord I made it down the isle. Thank God my cousin Roberto proudly stepped up for his late uncle and escorted me down the isle. It was a day I will always fondly remember...

PASTOR KEN HOUGHTON. "Dearly beloved, we are gathered here today to witness the union of this man and this woman in holy matrimony..." Yes, that's how it all started—all lovey dovey. Everyone smiled as they watched two people make a commitment that will be the battle of their lives. It's on now! Shane isn't ready yet. I ought to know. He's my son, just like me when I was his age—a true ladies man. Well, marriage will tame him. It certainly tamed me! Ha, ha! Shane is still out there checking out those fine young things. He should only have eyes for his new bride, and Shenir is about as angelic as you can get—raven black wavy hair down her back, olive skin, doe-like brown eyes and all that beauty contained in a perfect hour glass bottle—oh, to be 21 again! Shane doesn't know how blessed he is. I seen him eyeballing every girl that walked by him just today. I tried to convince him to wait, but he is as rebellious as his mother—never my way, always got to be June Houghton's way. Marriage is no cake walk, son!

SWEET "MAMASITA" SANCHEZ. Picture perfect is how I'd describe it. As Shenir and Shane sealed their wedding vows with a loving kiss, I was moved to tears. It reminded me of the day her father Christo and I wed, in spite of his Spanish family's objections to him marrying me, a beautiful dark-brown-skinned African American Queen—as my Mama would say! It took a while for his family to warm up to me, but once they got to know this real Black woman and after I gave birth to their first granddaughter, Shenir, they embraced me as one of their own. Christo affectionately called me his Mamasita from that day on. I'm so happy our beloved daughter Shenir finally found her Mr. Right. She would always say to me, "Mamasita, I know I found the one!" The two of them had dated off and on since college. My prayers were finally answered—and all that fasting—for these two to commit to one another, especially Shane. He couldn't seem to make up his mind between his high school sweetheart Mary Simpson and his college sweetheart, my lovely Shenir. Three years it took for him to finally propose. Shenir is truly one of the sweetest young Christian women. Shane's definitely blessed to have found my daughter. He seems to be a little tight on resources, though—always borrowing funds for this and for that. I practically fed him most of his adult life while they were in college. I wish his father was more financially supportive of this union. Maybe if Pastor Houghton could take his shifty green eyes off the young ladies prancing around him, he could see his own son's needs. Ken Houghton is as shameless as an old dusty brown pot-bellied hound dog in heat—and just as gruffy. Mrs. Houghton should shave him and put him in a cage before he bites one of the bride's maids. *Smile*. Well, it's been a rocky start for the two love birds, but I keep telling myself that as long as Shenir loves Shane, that's all that matters. I really wish them the best. Shenir and Shane are in God's hands now.

JUNE HOUGHTON. Shenir finally got her hooks into my son Shane. He's all wrapped around her little finger. I never could understand what Shaney saw in her. She didn't respect me enough. Always calling me by my first name,

June, since the first day she met me, no not ever First Lady Houghton. She didn't even want to join our church—said she was "spiritually grounded" at her own church home. Her mother should have taught her to be more respectful. But just look at her mother, excuse me, that's Mamasita. Some Nubian Diva she makes herself to be, dressed in a swirling dashiki with her thick black hair wrapped in a turban. She refers to herself as a "prophetess." Well, I pray for her and her whole mixed up looking family. As far as I'm concerned, Shenir is getting more than she deserves with my Shaney! He is full of promise. I know he hasn't actually graduated from college yet, but he will eventually. Maybe now that she has her degree, she can find a job and help him get his degree after all the love and support he's given her through college. I've got a lot of plans for my son. He will either be a pastor like his Daddy or maybe a doctor or a lawyer—when he makes up his mind and re-enters school. That little expulsion for fraternity hazing won't stop my Shaney. In the meantime, Shenir will just have to adjust and take good care of my boy. I've got to pray for these two, Lord!

SHANE HOUGHTON. I'll do all it takes to make this girl mine. Shenir is the cream in my coffee. I think I can do this, walk down the isle, say I do and whatever, give her a kiss. Then she's all mine. She'll have to honor and obey me. I always told her, "Good thing you can cook or this might not work out." I was just kidding, but then again I am glad she can cook. And those sweet starry brown eyes—well that helps too! You can't be with somebody if they can't please you. I'm tired of living at home with my parents. Yeah, I'm ready for this. It's been the "June and Pastor Houghton Show" way too long. My adoptive parents, I love them, but they have been molding me and shaping me like their own little piece of pottery since they took me in when I was seven. I don't remember my biological parents—I was told my mother left me at a fire station. I feel like the Preacher Kid Trophy, the Houghton's show piece. They're always putting me up on display at their storefront church, yes, *their* church—it's all about them. Mama June enters the church like she's a goddess. Her nose to the ceiling, my pleasingly plump—let her tell it—light-skinned rosy-cheeked Mama, always donned in a pastel-colored suit complete with matching wide-brimmed feathered hat—she's got eggshell, yellow, blue, pink, lavender and any other color of the rainbow you can imagine. She berates me right before we make our "first family" entrance, "Look good for the congregation, honey," "Smile for the deacon," or "Say yes ma'm to Mother so-and-so…" Ugh! I'd rather be at the club dancing with all the honeys. Well, it's time I get my own life. When Shenir got an apartment, I knew it was time for me to make my move. I had to get out of my parent's house, so I did what any thinking man would do, I proposed. Shenir grinned from ear to ear and said, "Yes!" I didn't even have a ring that day. I had to borrow $300.00 from my guy Dirksen and sale almost all my CD's—except for my rap—Dr. Dre and Snoop Dog, couldn't let my boys go—had those hidden in the basement! I finally scraped up just enough to get the wedding bands for today. Two simple silver bands, no big deal. Let's just do this thing. Shenir wouldn't have it any other way. "It's I do, or I don't," she'd always tell me. Well, I finally got my own Mrs. Houghton!

MIMI SANCHEZ. Ever since I can remember, Shenir wanted to get married. When we were little girls, she would draw pictures of herself in a wedding gown, draped in pearls, holding a bouquet of white flowers, with her long, silky black hair flowing in the wind. When she was 12 years old, one day after we watched Cinderella on television, she said "Mimi, I'm going to marry my soul mate and live happily ever after!" Well today, big sis, is certainly your day. A dream come true—Shane better be good to you! He seemed like an odd choice for her, though. Shenir's all into Jesus, a true Christian girl—church on Sunday, Bible study on Wednesday, choir rehearsal on Thursday, and mission groups throughout the month. She used to date collegiate types, *brainiacs* with braces and four-eyes. But Shane is a smooth operator, a laid back "player" type, although she met him in school. I remember when she brought him home to meet Daddy and Mamasita. Shane was the perfect gentleman at dinner. He kissed my mother's hand, pulled a chair for her to sit in, waited for us to sit down before he sat down. Daddy grilled him. "What are your intentions with my daughter?" he asked him. Shane just smiled and said that he intended to make her happy. Daddy didn't let him slide with that answer. He told Shane that Shenir was already happy and wanted to know how Shane could contribute to her happiness. Shenir gave me the eye, and I smiled back at her because we knew Shane had to pass "The Test" before Daddy would give his blessing for the two of them to be together. Shane simply said the only way to please a woman who has everything is to enjoy it with her and to support her in her own journey. That impressed Daddy but he still had one more question. "What about your education—without one, how will you *support* my daughter?" Shane promised my mother and father that he had every intention to re-enroll in school at a local college since he had been expelled from the university they attended and that he would build his own career from there. Shenir believed in him and that's what she told our parents that day. I hope one day I'll find my True Love.

VANESSA MONROE. Mmmmmmmm....This is such a lovely June day for Miss She She's wedding! All the birds are singing, the butterflies flying, the sun is shining and everything is just perrrrrfect...for *her*...yeah, good thing, too. I got the whole day figured out. Got my dress fitting all the right curves, and I'm ready to flirt. Ever since me and Dirksen broke up over that little kiss he shared with Shenir, I made up in my mind I'm never going to give my heart to one man. Shenir swore Dirksen caught her off guard that day at the pool last year. I had just walked away for a moment to the ladies room and when I returned their lips were locked together. He jumped back when I walked up. And Shenir backed up and wiped away his kiss, saying to me, "Vanessa, I'm so sorry—Dirksen came on to me." Yeah, eventually I forgave my girl, she was innocent as usual. But who could blame her? After all my Dirksen had everything a woman desired—lumberjack muscles on a dark chocolate frame and a smile that lit up the room. A real charismatic brother. He was even studying to be a preacher some day—a man with a heart for God, but not a heart for *me*. I sure can pick them. Me and Dirksen were on the brink of disaster anyway. He was too righteous—didn't want to party, didn't want to drink, didn't want to do anything that didn't start with Jesus! Shenir was just the perfect little excuse for me to get out of that dead end relationship with Dirksen. I had to cut him loose 'cause I have too much living to do. Party over here! Hope the single men are in the house today because Vanessa's got it going on! Miss She She may be ready to settle down forever and ever but I'm not! That's my best girl though, Miss Goody Goody. Honey, I've got to get out of this wedding scene so I can hit the club tonight. Hope those vows don't last forever, I mean, take forever to recite—*you know what I mean*. Cause I got to get my groove on! *Holla!*

DIRKSEN LANGLEY. There she goes, Miss Black-Spanish American Princess. I am still trying to digest the fact that Shenir is settling down with my dog, Shane. She got him to put away his player card—at least we hope that is the case. That should have been me walking down that isle. After all I had eyes on her first. She was like an angel from heaven when she entered Registration Hall on campus that first day of college. I told Shane, "Look, there goes the future Mrs. Dirksen Langley!" You know what he said? "Bet she'll be calling out my name from dusk 'til dawn before she can even say your name once!" Then Shane proceeded to march up to Shenir that day and introduce himself. He was just so arrogant. She ignored him at first. She was too good for him. It took him several weeks before he even got her to say "Hello" to him. Me, on the other hand, I had a different approach. I wanted to be her knight in shining armor. I became her good friend, no pressure. I was behind the scenes when Shenir broke up with the geeky guys she dated throughout college, a shoulder for her to cry on. I didn't sweat her and try to make her go out with me. She even set me up on a date with that crazy friend of hers, Vanessa—that didn't last long. I really just wanted Shenir. After all, if I'm going to preach, a man of the cloth needs a virtuous wife by his side. Shenir confided in me more than once that she was saving herself for Mr. Right. I still can't figure out how that became Shane. They're like night and day, water and oil, sugar and poison. Oh well, like Shenir would always say, the Lord works in mysterious ways.

ALONE WITH HIM

"Therefore, behold, I will allure her, and bring her into the wilderness, and speak comfortably unto her. And I will give her her vineyards from thence, and the valley of Achor for a door of hope: and she shall sing there, as in the days of her youth, and as in the day when she came up out of the land of Egypt. And it shall be at that day, saith the LORD, that thou shalt call me Ishi (that is my Husband); and shalt call me no more Baali (that is my Lord)."
—**Hosea 2:14-16 (KJV)**

Have you ever had a wilderness experience? It can be a time of great suffering—when your heart is broken by a loved one, or you're lonely, or you're battling an illness, or perhaps you're depressed. It's a time when you need to deal with yourself. But more importantly, it's a time when you need to reach out to the Lord. Why does God draw us into the wilderness? He desires a One-on-one relationship with each of us. It's in the wilderness where we draw close to Him for the comfort and security that we each need. It is in the wilderness where He shows Himself strong to us. There, it's just you and Him, alone. He has sanctified you and separated you for Himself for a season. And at that intimate moment, you realize, He is your True Love, your Heavenly Husband. That is when the wilderness becomes the *Secret Place*.

Chapter 1

Lovers Rock

"**SHANE, HONEY, YOU UP THERE?**" Shenir called out to her husband as she jogged up the stairs. Early from work, she was excited to be able to surprise her husband on a Friday afternoon. Shenir opened the master bedroom oak double doors.

"Oh, my God!" she screamed.

Shane and her best friend Vanessa were locked in a passionate embrace beneath the blue silk sheets her mother had given them for their fifth wedding anniversary. When Shane saw his wife Shenir standing in the doorway, he couldn't grab his pants fast enough as he jumped up out of the bed. Vanessa snatched the sheets from him to cover herself. Shane stood there speechless, his hazel eyes flashing back and forth wildly from Shenir to Vanessa.

Shenir fell against the mahogany wood-paneled wall for temporary support and began to cry and scream over and over, "Why? Why? Why?"

"Baby, it's not what you think, she don't mean anything to me," Shane said as he approached Shenir, trying to hold her. She tore herself away from him and lunged at Vanessa, yanking her out of the bed by her hair.

"Get out! Get out my house! I hate you!" yelled Shenir as tears streamed down her face.

Vanessa quickly grabbed her tan sundress which had been flung over the dresser and attempted to pull it over her head while trying to run out. Shenir caught the hem of Vanessa's dress and nearly ripped it off her before she got away. Shenir plopped on the floor and sat against the bed, hugging her knees and sobbing.

Shane stuttered as he tried to explain himself while tucking in his t-shirt. "Baby, it's not your fault. I just needed more love than you could give me," he managed.

She looked at him like he had lost his natural Black mind. Then she arose from the floor, proceeded to open the bedroom window and began snatching his clothes out the closet, tossing them out the second-story window. Shane grabbed her and tried to stop her. But she twisted from his grasp and slapped him hard to his astonishment. He stormed angrily out of the house, taking his car keys from the mantle as he left out the front door.

Heartbroken, Shenir sat on the edge of the bed and wept until her blouse was soaked. She could not believe what had just happened. The betrayal she felt overtook her like poison. And in that moment, she realized, she was alone, on her own, with a daughter to provide for, just like that.

"IT'S SO DARK IN HERE, Mommy. Will you turn the lights on—I can't sleep. I'm scared," said four-year old Zionna, just after her mother Shenir had switched the lights off for the night.

Even though the moonlight began to softly illuminate the room, Shenir could see the tears of fear building in her daughter's light brown eyes. Zionna's lip quivered slightly as she started to cry.

"Mommy, when is Daddy coming home?" she pouted.

"Zi, we talked about this. I told you that your father has gone away for a little while. Don't be afraid," said Shenir. It had been only seven days since that ugly scene with Shane and Vanessa. But the hardest part of it was trying to explain to her daughter that her parents were living apart. She could not forget how Zionna cried when her Daddy didn't come home that night.

"Can't you and Daddy just say you're sorry?" Zionna asked.

"Baby, it's just not that simple this time. Please understand, me and Daddy are not happy together."

Shenir tucked Zionna in bed, gently rubbing her forehead. "If you like, I'll turn on the closet light for you. Okay, honey?"

"All right, Mommy. But won't the closet monsters wake up?"

"Now who's been filling your head with all these scary stories about closet monsters?"

"Auntie Mimi told me last night that if she turned any lights on while I slept that closet monsters would wake up and eat me. Then she told me to close my eyes tight so they would think I was sleep and not mess with me."

"Zi, there's no such thing as closet monsters. Don't you know that Jesus wouldn't let anything like that hurt you?" Shenir clicked on the bedroom closet light.

"Will Jesus beat them up?"

"Honey, when Jesus is in the room, they don't even want to come in. They're afraid of Him."

"I thought you said they aren't real."

"Well, they're not."

"Is Jesus real, Mommy?"

"Yes He is."

"How do you know?"

"Because the Bible says so—that's how. Now you better get some sleep little girl or you won't be able to wake up early enough to see your favorite cartoons in the morning."

"Good night, Mommy."

"Good night, baby."

When Shenir left the room, Zionna began to pray:

"Jesus, please don't let the closet monsters eat me up. God bless Mommy, Auntie Mimi. And Jesus, if you know where my Daddy is, tell him that I miss him. Oh, and one more thing. Please let me see you, when you're ready to come out of hiding. Amen."

Zionna stared out the window from her bed. Hypnotized by the moonlight, she fell asleep. A few minutes later, Shenir peeked in the room and smiled at her slumbering little lady. Shenir laughed to herself about her daughter's inquisitiveness about Jesus. She'd always taught her daughter to believe in the Lord. Now Shenir was beginning to wonder maybe if she should teach Zionna more about the ways of the mysterious God Jehovah. *Tomorrow*, she thought, *I'll take Zi to Sunday school instead of waiting until morning service starts.*

EARLY THAT MORNING, Zionna woke up and ran to her mother's room. She shook Shenir frantically trying to wake her.

"Mommy, Mommy!"

"What, what's wrong Zi?" Shenir said groggily, yet startled.

"I saw Jesus!"

"What do you mean, honey? You had a dream?"

"It was real, Mommy. He talked to me. He told me that He loved me and you and Auntie Mimi and Daddy. He said Daddy's coming back too, Mommy! Daddy's coming back!

Jesus wanted me to tell you that you've got to take me to Sunday school today instead of waiting until church starts."

"Oh, my God—you—"

Shenir stared at her beaming child in disbelief, knowing full well she hadn't spoke out loud last night about taking Zionna to Sunday school. *Maybe, this is some weird coincidence*, she thought.

"Honey, what did Jesus look like?" she asked testing her daughter.

"Oh, Mommy, He's beautiful! He glows. And His smile made me feel warm all over! Hurry up, Mommy. We've got to get to Sunday school *this* morning!"

"What about all your cartoons, Zi?" she chided, while smiling at her little girl.

"No, Mommy, we've got to go—*now!*" Zionna tugged at her mother's arm, trying to pull her out of bed.

"All right, all right. Let me find you something to wear." Shenir arose and went into Zionna's room with her daughter skipping behind her.

"Ooh, Mommy, can I wear this dress," Zionna pleaded as she pulled at the pink frilly cotton dress complete with a feather boa.

"No, Zionna, that dress is for special occasions only."

"Please, Mommy, church is a special occasion—please, please, please?"

"Well, I guess it will be ok, honey," Shenir said, not wanting to discourage her daughter. "I'll agree, but only if you promise not to run around church playing in it."

"I promise."

A few minutes later, Shenir hummed softly as she ironed Zionna's favorite pink dress. She still couldn't get over her daughter telling her that her Daddy was coming back. Shenir literally had not seen Shane again since the day he left. His mother, Mama June, called Shenir later that night to find out what had happened. Apparently, Shane had arrived at

Kiss The Son

his mother's house drunk, collapsed on her sofa and passed out. Shane called Shenir every night for the next few days, but she just hung up on him every time. She vowed that she would never forgive him and Vanessa. Tears began to well up in her eyes as she reflected on the day that her whole world had changed. Her heart was still very tender. Shenir finished pressing her daughter's pink dress for church.

"Are you okay, Mommy?" Zionna asked as she tugged at the bottom of Shenir's skirt.

"I'm fine, baby. Here's your dress. Let's get you ready Little Miss Lady!"

THAT MORNING THE RAIN was falling in a light mist—just enough to make a sistah's hair go back. Shenir tied her hair up in a shimmering lilac silk rain scarf as she prepared to head out for Sunday school. Zionna was covered from head to nearly her toes in a shiny purple rain coat with matching cap, carrying a tiny multi-colored umbrella that opened up like the wings of a butterfly. Shenir brushed some lint off her navy-blue velvet form-fitting dress and threw on her raspberry rain poncho, taking her little girl by the hand as they walked toward the car parked in the driveway. With a beep of her key alarm, she unlocked the automatic locks and they hopped in her red sedan.

Shenir drove eastbound a few miles down the road to Shekinah Glory Christian Center located on the south side of Chicago. They arrived promptly at 9:00 a.m., and Shenir checked their coats in at the entrance. She dropped her daughter off at the children's Sunday school class in the Lambs of Zion Room, and she went to the Good Shepherd Room for adult Sunday school down the hall.

"Good morning everyone," said Minister Lisa Tucker, the Sunday school teacher for the adult class. "The lesson today is on 'Forgiveness and Reacceptance.'"

Shenir almost fell out of her seat. Everyone turned and looked as she regrouped. *The Lord must really be trying to tell me something today*, she thought, as she turned to the assigned scripture, Matthew 6:14-15.

"Would you like to read this morning, Sister Shenir?" said Minister Tucker with a tender smile.

Shenir began reading, "For if ye forgive men their trespasses, your Heavenly Father will also forgive you: But if ye forgive not men their trespasses, neither will your Father forgive your trespasses."

"Amen. How many of you here have ever had someone do something to you that you couldn't imagine forgiving because it was so bad?"

A few people raised their hands, but Shenir did not move. She did not want to talk about her recent break up with Shane in front of everyone in class.

"Now, I'm sure that there are more of you, but perhaps you'd rather not discuss it right now. Well, I'm here to tell you today that if you can't tell me about it, you've got to confess it to the Father because if He's willing to forgive the world of all the wicked things we've done, surely the least you can do is forgive someone else. After all, we are not greater than our God!"

A flurry of amen's filled the room.

"It is a sin to carry around an unforgiving spirit. In Romans 6:16, the Word says: 'Know ye not, that to whom ye yield yourselves servants to obey, his servants ye are to whom ye obey; whether of sin unto death, or of obedience unto righteousness?'" recited Minister Tucker. "I ask you class, who are you obeying? For those who can't bury the hatchet, you just might get cut. You're here on this earth to obey, serve and please the Lord. Carrying around a grudge can come between you and the Father—get rid of the garbage, y'all, and clean up the pipeline of communication between you and God. Because if your life is full of sin, it's like static in the telephone when you pray to the Lord."

"Like when your cell phone drops?" chimed a sister from the back of the classroom.

"That's right! And we don't want to lose our connection with Jesus!" blurted a man seated by the window and everyone laughed.

"Who wants to be closer to the Father?" asked the minister.

Everyone raised their hands at this point.

"Take your commitment to the Lord to the next level. Forgive your brother, your sister, your husband, your wife or whoever it is that wronged you. And I guarantee that the misery you feel now will be washed away. If you can't do it face to face, start where it counts the most—in your heart. Amen?"

Amen's cascaded through the classroom. Shenir stood up with the class and bowed her head as they linked up hand-in-hand in prayer. Minister Tucker led the prayer:

"Heavenly Father:

We honor You and bless Your name. Lord, we thank You for teaching us today about forgiveness. We come to You as humbly as we know how. Lord we ask for You to bless us with a forgiving spirit. Let us not cling to the past, nor the worries of this world O Master. But let us bind the fleshly barriers that come between You and Your people, O God. Take away the bitterness of unforgiveness and sin and replace it with your sweet joy and everlasting love. Merciful God, Jehovah Jireh, our Provider, we praise You for we know that You are able to keep us from falling. Straighten us out Father God. Fix us who are broken. Create in us a clean heart and renew in us a right spirit. Make us new and beautiful servants of

Yours O Most High God. We ask these things in the name of Your Beloved Only Begotten Son, our Lord and Savior Jesus Christ. Amen."

Shenir left out of class feeling as if a burden had been lifted off of her. Although she felt the hurt of Shane's unfaithfulness lingering inside of her, she felt the urge to see him and forgive him. Still she wondered, if she took him back whether he would cheat on her again. She knew her heart could not take it if he did. Shenir understood now that she had to forgive him even if they did not get back together.

SHENIR DROVE HOME THAT SUNDAY afternoon as Zionna lay sleeping in her booster car seat in the backseat. The combination of Zionna's light snoring, the falling September raindrops and the swishing of the windshield wipers was beginning to make Shenir drowsy. She switched on her car radio and turned to FM WWJD the all-the-time dusty station. She came to a stop at the red light as "Reasons," by Earth, Wind and Fire, serenaded her softly from the speakers. She began to hum along with the lyrics as she reflected on the last good time she had with her husband. It was their fifth wedding anniversary, just last June 2, 2005. They decided to spend a quiet evening at home. Shenir brought home an exquisite Italian dinner from Sicily's Secret restaurant earlier that day to heat up for the two of them. Her sister Mimi was babysitting Zionna at her apartment, and romance was definitely in the air at the Houghton's house.

Shenir heated up the shrimp fettuccine with alfredo sauce on the stove and drizzled melted herb butter onto the toasted garlic rolls. While in the living room, Shane sorted through their music love collection. He chose Sade's sultry *Lovers Rock* CD and played the title track softly in the background. Shane entered the kitchen and gently caressed Shenir around her waist, turning her toward him for a moment of romantic slow dancing. As she gazed into his soulful eyes, he began to plant gentle kisses on her face.

"You look fine tonight, Mrs. Houghton," he said in a deep, husky voice that made her heart melt.

"You're not so bad yourself, Mr. Houghton," Shenir laid her head on his chest as they danced the night away.

That's how it was between the two of them just three months ago. Tears ran down Shenir's cheek as she tried to understand the *reasons*—like the song chimed—why Shane could have possibly cheated on her with her so-called best friend. Jealousy and raging emotions overtook her, defeating her earlier desire to forgive Shane. *How could he do that to me?*

LATER THAT EVENING when the telephone rang, Shenir, who had fallen asleep on the living room sofa, woke up and picked up the receiver.

"Hello Shenir, this is Dirksen. How are you?" said her and Shane's old friend from college.

"Dirksen? Is this really you?" Shenir asked.

"I know it has been a while, but you and Shane were in my spirit, so I thought I'd call and see how you both were doing. How's my guy?"

"Wow, it's been a while since I heard from you. What have you been doing since you and Shane's fishing trip last year?" she said, trying to change the subject.

"Well, actually, I've been focusing on my ministry. I have begun my own flock of about fifty members down at the YMCA on Stony Island. We meet Sunday evenings at seven o'clock," said Dirksen.

Shenir remembered how Dirksen used to tell her he would be a pastor when they were in college five years ago. He would stand up in the front of the dorm hall and pretend like he was giving his first sermon, clear his throat and begin to preach like nobody's business.

"You always did say you'd start your own church," said Shenir. "That must be nice."

"Why don't you and Shane stop by next Sunday night and support me," Dirksen smiled and could hardly contain himself. "This is my first official sermon as Pastor of the United Disciples For Christ. Please come by. It would be so nice to see you both."

"Dirksen, I must tell you. Shane and I broke up."

"Oh, Shenir, I'm so sorry to hear that. Are you okay?"

"About as well as can be expected."

"That's why you both were in my spirit. Shenir, I'm going to pray for you," he said, longing to comfort her. "Is there anything you need? What about Zionna, how is she holding up?"

"She has really been missing her Daddy," Shenir broke off, choking back her tears. She took a deep breath. "Well, I really must be going now. Maybe I'll stop by on Sunday and hear a young brother preach, okay?"

"Okay, Shenir. You take care of yourself and stay sweet. Good night." Dirksen hung up the telephone and sat stunned for a moment. He could not believe the couple had broken up. He just knew it had to be something that Shane did, not Shenir. He prayed silently for his friends.

LOVER OF MY SOUL

"...I found Him whom my soul loveth: I held Him, and would not let Him go."
"My Beloved is mine, and I am His..."
—Song of Solomon 3:4; 2:16 (KJV)

Our hearts ache for true romance. Some of us go through life seeking that special someone, going through breakup after breakup. Once we find our "soul mate," we think that's it, only to awaken to the fact that our lover is not perfect. The reality is...none of us are perfect—none but Jesus, He is perfect. It is when you accept Jesus as your Lord and Savior and ask Him into your heart that you engage in a loving dance with the Lover of your soul. Having looked everywhere for the perfect lover, you can now find Him in the *Secret Place* of your heart.

Chapter 2

Part-Time Lovers

HE SHOWED UP LATE as usual. Mimi wondered why she even bothered to meet up with her date Marco Ortiz. He wasn't really her type. She was a fun-loving, short curly-haired 21-year-old fashionista. Her Spanish blood accentuated her Afrocentric flava. Marco, on the other hand, was a young athletic Puerto Rican man who was a bar hopper by night and an accountant by day. To top it off, he had the nerve to always expect her to sit around Club Connection waiting for him at the bar while he took his time. What in the world did she ever see in him? Nevertheless, she waited. *Better than no one at all*, she thought.

"Hey sexy lady, can I hook up with you?" said a heavy set light-skinned Black man who was walking by the bar. Tattoos of guns brazed the bright olive tone of his muscular upper arms.

"I'm chillin' right now, waiting on my friend," Mimi said. She coolly swept back the black curly bangs from her eyes.

"My name is Tim. You mind if I wait with you a while?" Tim asked as he sat down beside her. Mimi nodded, and the man ordered his drink. "Joe Bean, my man, give me a shot of Bourbon."

"Coming right up, Officer," said the bartender.

"And what will you have sweetheart?" the man asked Mimi.

"No thanks," Mimi refused his offer, not wanting to sign his unwritten contract.

"It's just a drink love. Why don't you join me for a taste?"

"Look, I said no thanks," she retorted.

Just then Marco came into the bar dressed in black jeans, a white button up and blue silk tie. His stocky build, light brown sun-tanned skin and straight jet black hair commanded attention when he entered a room. He walked up to Mimi and put his arm around her waste in an attempt to rescue his "damsel in distress."

"What's up my man? You can't take no for an answer?" asked Marco in his deep Spanish accent.

"Hey, she was on me since I walked in the place. She wants me, and I know how to treat a lady," said Tim.

"She's taken." Marco responded.

"Look, she said she was waiting on a *friend*. That be *you*?"

"Well—I," Marco stuttered, unsure of himself. "You sure ain't her friend, so get off her case!"

"It's a free country! Why don't *you* get off her case seeing that you're just a *friend*!" Tim mocked.

"Mimi, let's go," Marco said, as he placed Mimi's brown leather bomber jacket around her shoulders.

Tim grabbed Mimi's sleeve before Marco could finish putting it on her.

"She ain't goin' nowhere!" the officer said as he forced Mimi back into her seat.

Marco swung at Tim, but Tim ducked then gutter punched him. Marco socked Tim in the jaw. Then Tim recovered and bulldozed Marco into the table behind him, knocking drinks everywhere.

Mimi was screaming. "Stop! Stop it!"

But the men were out of control. The next thing Mimi knew, a herd of Chicago's Finest rushed into the bar. By then, there were many others fighting, chairs were flying, people were running out of the bar. The date was a total disaster.

The police handcuffed Marco and arrested him for assaulting Officer Tim. But Tim wasn't hauled away in a paddy wagon like Marco. Wiping blood from his swollen lip, Tim staggered back to the bar to finish his drink. Mimi quickly exited before he noticed she was leaving. She left out the back door and got in her sky blue SUV and sped off, still trembling and shaken from the bar fight.

"Lord God, when will I ever find the right man?" she muttered under her breath as she drove home, tears streaming down her face. Then she cried out, "I can't take this anymore! I just can't!"

MIMI PULLED INTO THE PARKING LOT of her apartment complex and parked her SUV near the apartment entrance. She hopped out, slamming the car door and entered her building, running up the stairs to the second floor. When Mimi got home Saturday night after her hell date, the night was still young. There were three messages on her answering machine. She tossed her leather jacket on the dinette chair, kicked off her Stilettos and flopped on a throw pillow on the floor. She hit play on her answering machine and checked her messages. The first message was from her older sister, Shenir.

"Mimi, I've got some good news. Call me when you get home—it's about Mamasita."

The next message was from their mother.

"I heard from the doctor today. Please call me, honey."

After the beep, the next message was a hang up call.

"I wonder who *that* was," Mimi blurted as she saw the caller ID listed it as a blocked call. It had only been three months since the burglary. A man had broken into her apartment while she was asleep and stolen her purse and some of her jewelry. He was on his way out the window when she woke up and screamed. He escaped. She was totally freaked out by the incident. The police told her it was a good thing that he only wanted her belongings and that anything could have happened to her. She wondered about the burglar because something about him had looked very familiar. Although the burglar was wearing a ski mask, he had a scar on his right arm similar to the one that John, an old boyfriend of hers, had. When she had broken up with John, he didn't take it very well. In fact, he threatened her, telling her that she had not seen the last of him. Since then she had gotten an alarm system and stopped sleeping with her windows open.

It was only 9 o'clock, so Mimi decided to call her mother back.

"Hi, Mamasita."

"Mimi—hold on a minute, baby. Shenir's on the other line. I'll put us on a three-way call," said her mother as she switched over the calls.

"What's up, Shenir?"

"Hey, Mimi!"

"Girls, I've got some good news," said Mamasita. "The doctor called me this afternoon and said he couldn't wait to give me the good news—bless his heart! He said that my last chemotherapy session was a success. The breast cancer has gone into remission!"

"Praise the Lord!" Shenir shouted.

"Oh, Mamasita, I'm so happy!" said Mimi.

"And there's more," Mamasita said, "I won't be needing the mastectomy after all. The disease was caught in time before it spread too far."

"The Lord answered our prayers," said Shenir. "I'm so glad, Mamasita. Thank you, Jesus!"

"Yes Lord! Shenir, I've been praying for you too, chile'— for you and Shane and Zionna," said their mother.

"I'm doing all right. Please don't worry," said Shenir.
"Has he called you?" asked Mimi.
"Yes, but I haven't taken his calls," said Shenir.
Shenir sure is trying to sound all nonchalant about her marital problems, thought Mimi.
"He should be calling you to kiss your feet," retorted Mimi. "If he was *my* man, I'd make him beg until he was blue in the face!"
"Now, Mimi, don't be so hard on your big sister. She's got to deal with this in her own way. Sugar, are you going to be all right?"
"Yes, Ma. Don't worry yourself about it. Okay?"
"Shenir, you don't sound like yourself," said Mimi, sensing the brokenness in her sister's voice. "Maybe, I should come by there and keep you company."
"Suit yourself, sis. You know you're always welcome," said Shenir.
"I'll be right over to help you shake off those blues. See ya!"
"All right, Shenir, you give my granddaughter Zionna a big kiss. Now, you girls have some fun and don't be over there having no pity party either. Bye!"
"Yes, M'am. Bye." Shenir and Mimi chorused, and they all hung up.

WHEN MIMI ARRIVED at her sister's house, little Zionna was sound asleep. Shenir hung Mimi's coat in the front coat closet, then she carried Zionna to her bedroom. "I'll be back downstairs in a sec' Mimi," Shenir grunted as she hauled the little girl to her room. Shenir laid Zionna down in her bed and gave her daughter a kiss. "That's from Nana," Shenir whispered.
Shenir went into the kitchen and grabbed a frozen gourmet pizza out the freezer.

"I know pepperoni supreme is one of your favorites, Mimi—with all the toppings."

"Yeah girl you know that's me. Hook it up!" said Mimi as she thumbed through Shenir's DVD collection for a late night movie.

Shenir placed the pizza on a long baking sheet and put it in the oven for 20 minutes.

"I didn't know you had *Officer And A Gentleman*," exclaimed Mimi. "I love that movie. What I wouldn't do to have my Prince Charming come and rescue me from my job!"

"Still searching to find the one?" asked Shenir.

"You know me, girl. There's just nothing out there for me. I had a horrible date tonight with Marco. He ended up in jail after a bar brawl with a policeman."

"Sounds like loads of fun," Shenir said.

"Shenir, I am really about to give up."

"You know what you need, Mimi? A good dose of spirit-filled fellowship."

"What do you mean?"

"Well, my church has a women's Bible study group that I hear is off the chain for single and divorced women. It's called Heavenly Prince Bible Study Group, and it starts the same time as regular Sunday School."

"Maybe so, I don't know," said Mimi as she slipped into the bathroom.

Just then the oven timer and the doorbell were going off at the same time. Since Mimi was in the restroom, Shenir turned the oven and the timer off and went up front to open the door. There stood her husband Shane carrying a giant Marshall Field's shopping bag.

"Shane," Shenir paused for a moment trying to regain her composure from the shock of seeing him again. "What are you doing here?"

"Look, I know you don't want to see me, but I came to see Zionna."

"She's sleep, Shane. It's after 10 o'clock," she said sharply.

"Well, wake her up. I really want to see her."

"You should of thought about that before you started creeping."

"Shenir, you can't keep me from seeing my daughter. You always hang up the phone when I call. You won't let me talk to her, let alone talk to you, on the phone. I couldn't just stay away forever. I need to see Zionna."

"Haven't you done enough to hurt us, Shane?"

"Sooner or later, you're going to have to let me see her. She is *my* daughter too."

"Daddy!" Zionna's high-pitched shrill resounded as she bounded down the stairs running to her father's awaiting arms.

"Hey, Pumpkin!" Shane's eyes lit up as he lifted her off her little feet. "Did you miss me?"

"Yes, Daddy. Why won't you come back home?"

"Ask your Mommy."

"That's unfair Shane!" shouted Shenir as she stormed out of the living room and entered the kitchen. She was too angry to be in the same room with him.

"Did I hear *Shane?* Is he here?" Mimi whispered with disgust as she came out the restroom and came back into the kitchen. Shenir nodded, looking visibly shaken.

Shane was acting as if nothing had ever happened, Shenir noticed as she watched him and Zionna from the kitchen. He was laughing and playing with Zionna, and their daughter was grinning like it was Christmas.

Shenir began to cry as she slumped into a soft brown leather kitchen chair. She rested her head on the table and silently she prayed, *Oh Lord, why is my life so upside down. Why did all this have to happen? I'd have to be a straight* up fool to forgive him. He'd just think he could do what he wanted to me. What should I do?

"Mommy's not happy anymore since you went to stay with Grandma June," said the four-year-old.

"Well, maybe I'll come home soon, baby girl."

"Carry me piggyback, Daddy! Let me have a ride—please, please, please?"

"Okay, climb aboard the Sooooul Train!" laughed Shane as Zionna climbed on his back. After the quick ride, Shane reached into the shopping bag he'd brought and handed Zionna a pretty pink teddy bear.

"I like it, Daddy!" Zionna began to play with the bear's floppy ears.

Shane left Zionna in the living room for a moment, promising her he'd be right back. He came into the kitchen and stood in the doorway. Mimi rolled her eyes at her brother-in-law and left out the kitchen to play with Zionna.

Shenir lifted up her head and met Shane's glance. *He certainly hasn't lost his good looks*, she thought as she gazed at him. *Still, why was something that was supposed to be all mine given away so easily by him?*

Shane approached her, touching her arm gently before speaking.

"You never gave me a chance to tell you that I was sorry. I am, you know. I never meant to hurt you, Shenir. I really love you."

They were eye-to-eye as he knelt beside her and took her hand. Tears welled up in his eyes as he looked at her waiting for her response.

"How can I ever trust you again?" She moaned and cupped her face with her hands, wiping her tears away.

"Let me earn your trust back, Shenir. I'll repay every tear you shed, I promise."

Shenir looked away from him but deep inside she longed to forgive her husband.

"Please take me back, baby. I won't hurt you again. I'm really sorry."

He was crying, something she had never seen him do in front of her in all the five years that they had been married. He always held it together for both of them, no matter what the circumstances were.

"Why did you hurt me, Shane?"

"I wasn't trying to hurt you baby. I was weak and one thing led to another."

"But I thought what we had was special, Shane. At least, you used to tell me that."

"Our relationship is very precious to me, Shenir. I will always, always love you."

Just then, little Zionna burst into the kitchen like a ball of energy and began tugging at his sleeve.

"Daddy, Daddy! Come play with me!" little Zionna demanded.

"Soon, sweetheart, soon. Ok, but not right now," he answered as he stood up. Then he picked Zionna up and kissed her on her forehead.

"Daddy's got to go now." Shenir led him out.

Zionna started crying and screaming. "Daddy don't go—don't go, Daddy please—stay!" She burrowed her face into his chest and clung to his shirt.

Shenir pried Zionna from Shane's arms as she cried. As Shane opened the front door, Mimi walked back toward the kitchen, looking at Shane like he was public enemy number one. Shane left out, got into his army green Range Rover and drove away. Shenir calmed Zionna, kissing her on the forehead, then sent her back upstairs to her bedroom to play with her new teddy bear.

"What's going on, Shenir?" asked Mimi as Shenir entered the kitchen.

"He came to apologize."

"Well, what are you going to do?"

"I don't know right now. I really don't know, Mimi."

"I was trying to be cool in front of Zionna," Mimi smirked. "But, girl, I thought I was going to run upside that fool's head for what he did to you! You do still have that Louisville slugger in your closet, don't you?" Just five years younger than Shenir, Mimi didn't take no mess.

"Mimi, you have a lot to learn about love," Shenir laughed.

"Never mind me! It's hard to find a good man. I think I may check out that Heavenly Prince Bible Study Group, and you ought to come with me, Shenir."

"Well, I know Jesus loves me," said Shenir. "It's Shane's love I'm doubtful about."

"You *still* love him after all he's done?" asked Mimi. "Seems like it's starting to get to him—you two not being together. Maybe, it's getting to you too, huh Shenir?"

"Look, I said I don't know what I'm going to do. Okay? Let's just leave it at that."

"All right, calm down, sis," Mimi said as she peeked in the oven. "Shoot, I'm ready to eat a slice of this pizza and watch me a movie!"

"You go ahead. I'm not hungry anymore."

THE NEXT MORNING AT CHURCH Mimi gave Shenir a hug and kissed little Zionna as they each went off into their own Sunday School classes. Mimi went to the Heavenly Prince Bible Study Group held in the lunch room down the hall.

Mimi entered the classroom and sat in the rear. Although she had not yet joined Shekinah Glory Christian Center, she was curious about the class her sister referred her to. *I tried everything else to find Mr. Right, so seeking the Lord's help couldn't hurt*, she thought.

"Good morning ladies. I'm Cheryl Stevens and just like some of you, I was in search of Mr. Right," said the petite, short-haired brown-skinned teacher as she dramatically placed the back of her right hand to her forehead in a woe-is-me gesture. Everyone in the room laughed. She walked up to the blackboard and wrote a scripture in pink chalk:

Ezekiel 16:8-14
"When Mr. Right Finds You"

"I used to go to bars every Friday and Saturday night," said Cheryl. "Each time I'd go, I would meet a different man, we'd talk and have a drink and sometimes we'd leave the bar."

Cheryl looked straight out at the audience of single and divorced women. Without blinking, she confessed, "And sometimes, I wouldn't come home. This became a ritual for me. That was, until Mr. Right found me. I was seated at my favorite bar drinking a margarita and smoking a cigarette. A lady sat down next to me and handed me a Bible tract entitled: Looking For Mr. Right? His Name is Jesus. That lady lead me to the Lord right there in the bar. In fact, she's right in this room with us—please bless my co-teacher ya'll!"

The teacher's eyes began to tear up and a tissue was handed to her by the young Asian-American co-teacher seated in the first row. Cheryl's jaws tightened as she pulled herself together, she dried her eyes, and then put her hands on her hips and smiled.

"He found me in my mess and turned my life around." Cheryl pointed to Mimi, "You, in the back, what's your name?"

"Mimi."

"Mimi, please read Ezekiel 16:8."

Mimi cleared her throat and read the scripture to the class: "Now when I passed by thee, and looked upon thee, behold, thy time was the time of love; and I spread my skirt over thee, and covered thy nakedness: yea, I sware unto thee, and entered into a covenant with thee, saith the Lord GOD, and thou becamest mine."

Cheryl then added, "Before the Lord found Jerusalem, she was a hot mess, a newborn sinner lying in her own blood. No one cared about her until He took an interest in her and made her His own."

The co-teacher arose and handed out cards, each bearing an act of the LORD noted in the scripture of the day. "Every week, we will discuss one of the Lord's loving acts toward His betrothed. We will discuss The Covering, The Covenant, His Washing, The Anointing, Being Clothed In Christ, Girded In Truth, Bejeweled By The Beloved, Crowned For Reigning, Beautified For His Pleasure and Perfected Daily."

Mimi was enthralled in the lesson as Cheryl continued teaching on The Covering and how love covered a multitude of sins when Christ died on the cross. Mimi now understood why her sister told her the class was so great.

"Jesus wants to cover your sins, cover your shame and cover your life with His glory," said Cheryl. "Just like He did with Jerusalem, He wants to be your Covering. He will not leave you exposed. Once you are covered in the Blood of the Lamb, you will be purified in His sight and He can enter into a Covenant Relationship with you as His bride."

"Will there be a wedding?" asked a frail golden-haired white woman in the back.

"Yes," answered Cheryl. "Let's look at Revelation 19:7."

The golden-haired lady began to read:

"Let us be glad and rejoice, and give honor to Him: for the marriage of the Lamb is come, and His wife hath made herself ready."

"Ladies, we must make ourselves ready for Jesus! The Lord will help us, but we have to be willing to receive His help and follow His commandments," Cheryl said. "The only question is, what are you willing to give up so that you can receive so much more under the Covering of Christ?"

The class was silent as Cheryl discussed acts of sacrifice. The teacher then separated the students into breakout groups of four, so that the ladies could share their stories with one another. While there were no men in the class, Mimi found it interesting to share her thoughts and feelings about relationships with the other women in the group.

"I have had one upside down relationship after another," confessed Mimi to the ladies in her group. "I've gone to bars, dated friends, been on blind dates, but I had no idea that the Lord cared about me this way."

Mimi thought that she was alone in her search for the perfect mate. Now she realized that life was not all about finding a man, but she was beginning to realize that the Lord designed her for a destiny. Many women began sharing their testimonies. Mimi knew she would return to the Bible study group.

SHENIR ASKED MIMI to watch Zionna for her that Sunday evening, so she could go and hear Dirksen preach at the YMCA. Shenir entered the gymnasium at the YMCA shortly after seven o'clock and the church service had already begun. The fifty or so members and guests were on their feet in praise, singing Shout To The Lord. Everyone in the gymnasium was clapping their hands and praising God. Shenir spotted Dirksen in the front row and made eye contact with him as she waived and took a seat near the back.

About 10 minutes later, Dirksen stepped up to the makeshift pulpit on the stage in the gym and began to give his sermon.

"Go with me to the Book of John, Chapter 14, Verse 12. Let us read:

"'Verily, verily, I say unto you, He that believeth on Me, the works that I do shall he do also; and greater works than these shall he do; because I go unto my Father.'"

A young woman who was seated in the front brought a cup of water and a small white towel up to the pulpit and quietly placed them at Dirksen's fingertips. He mouthed a thank you and she returned to her seat.

"Today's sermon is entitled, 'A Greater Work,'" said Dirksen. "How can anyone do anything greater than the LORD? No one is greater than God. He parted the Red Sea, walked on water, rose from the dead. Is there a *catch*?" Dirksen furrowed his bushy eyebrows, pursed his lips and shook his head from side to side. The congregation laughed.

"When asked to do something new, something scary or something more than you normally do, how do you react? Some are excited, some become paralyzed with fear, some just procrastinate, while others get it done." He wiped his brow with the small white towel.

"Are you a doer? The Lord commands us in His Word to be doers of the Word and not just hearers of the Word. But, how do you do greater?" Dirksen took a sip of water from the cup before him.

"With God all things are possible!" he shouted. "In First John, Chapter 4, Verse 4, the Word says, 'Ye are of God, little children, and have overcome them: because greater is he that is in you, than he that is in the world.' Now stay with me, I'm going somewhere."

Dirksen paced back and forth, adjusted the mouthpiece to his headset. He cupped his chin with his right hand and put his forefinger to his lips, looking up in thought. "Jesus was in the world at the time—not of the world, mind you, but in the world. But now that you have received Him as Lord, He is in you! He is Greater—all power has been given to Him in heaven and in earth—see Matthew 28:18. He is Lord of the living and the dead—that's in Romans 14:9. And you can do all things through Christ who strengthens you—see Philippians 4:13. You can do greater works because the greater One lives in you! Somebody shout Hallelujah!"

Churchgoers were up on their feet shouting and clapping.

"When someone asks you if you can do better, if you feel better or tells you that you better do something—you tell them, 'I can do greater—nothing is impossible! Praise Jesus!" Dirksen was hopping and praising the Lord with all his heart and raising his hands to glorify God.

Shenir was on her feet shouting. She knew that she could do anything even in the midst of her storm. She cried out, "Glory!" Shenir was so happy that she came to hear Dirksen give his sermon. Then she heard a soft voice inside of her whisper, *Is he not the one?*

DREAM MAKER

"The prophet that hath a dream, let him tell a dream; and he that hath My word, let him speak My word faithfully. What is the chaff to the wheat? saith the LORD. Is not My word like as a fire? saith the LORD; and like a hammer that breaketh the rock in pieces?"
—Jeremiah 23:28-29 (KJV)

Have you ever awakened from a bad dream only to realize all was well? Sometimes life can seem like a nightmare until the Lord works the problem out. That's when victory is yours for the taking. Enjoy every moment, enjoy the good times and embrace them. Our Lord is the Maker Of Dreams. He is the One who gives us life, vision and prosperity. The troubles in life make us strong. We must endure until the good dreams start to unfold. We must wait on the Lord to make our hopes and dreams come true. He will, according to His will.

Chapter 3

Broken Pieces

"SHENIR, WHEN YOU GET IN TOMORROW MORNING, I need to meet with you to go over the Simpson case. The hearing is at noon, and I need you to help me complete an answer to a petition," said Attorney Samuel King, over the telephone intercom. Shenir clicked through her computer files as she sat at her cubicle at the Law Offices of King & Thomas, Ltd., looking for a petition she had prepared for Sam last month for a different divorce client. She wanted to review it to see how the client's divorce case applied to her own pending marriage. It was nearly 5:00 p.m., and the Monday workday was coming to an end, so she gave up the search and grabbed her jacket and purse.

"Okay Sam," she responded over the intercom. "Should I arrive a little earlier than nine?" she asked, hoping he'd turn down the offer. Sam had always been understanding of her job hours because of her child. Shenir had been a paralegal for the firm for the past two years.

"Well, actually if you could that would be great, since I'm meeting with another client at ten o'clock. Would you mind coming in at 8:30 a.m. rather than nine o'clock? I'll pay you for the overtime," Sam offered.

"No problem. I'll see you in the morning, Sam," Shenir replied respectfully, wondering if the new petition might be similar to the one she was looking for earlier. Still, she thought, maybe it was for the best that she didn't find it, since she wasn't very sure if she was going to proceed with getting a divorce. In a state of confusion about her conflicting feelings toward Shane, she promised herself she'd pray about it later that evening. As she reached Julianna's receptionist desk on her way out, a delivery man entered the office carrying a dozen roses.

"Delivery for Attorney Regina Thomas," said the balding gray-haired elderly black man. Then he flashed a smile at Juliana, "Sign here, please."

After the delivery man left, Julianna tossed her shoulder-length blonde hair behind her ears and peeked at the card standing in the flowers. She bucked her green eyes and smirked. "Regina's husband is always sending her flowers. I wish my man would be that thoughtful."

"Guess I won't be getting any roses anytime soon either," Shenir sighed.

"Girl please, Mr. Thomas is just trying to get on her good side. Probably wants something," retorted Julianna.

"Ain't that the truth!" Shenir blurted and they burst out laughing. "See you in the morning, Miss Julianna."

WHEN SHENIR ARRIVED AT HOME, Mimi was there with Zionna. As a routine, she always picked up Zionna from preschool for Shenir.

"Look, Mommy! Look!" shouted Zionna as she thrust a drawing proudly at her mother. "I did it in school. It's you, me and Daddy—just like before Daddy left!"

"Honey, that's nice."

"Can I put it on the 'frigerator, Mommy?"

Reluctantly, but not wanting to disappoint her little artist, Shenir posted the drawing on the refrigerator under the daisy magnet. Mimi noticed the strained look on her sister's face and just shook her head as she got ready to leave.

"Give Auntie a kiss!" shouted Mimi. Zionna rushed to Mimi's extended arms and gave her a huge hug and smooch. "See you tomorrow, Poch."

"Bye bye Auntie Mimi!" chimed Zionna.

Later that evening, as Shenir prepared beef stew for dinner, she stared at the picture on the refrigerator. The family scene with a bright sunshine and smiling stick people, two big ones and one little one all holding hands, was hardly a reality. The child's smile was the biggest with large teeth grinning back at her. Just then the telephone rang.

"Hello, Shenir?" said a deep husky voice.

Shenir recognized Shane's baritone right away.

"Hi Shane," she said flatly.

"I was wondering if it would be alright if I stopped by tonight. I bought Zionna a gift and I'd like to give it to her if I can?"

"Yeah, but why tonight? It's only Monday, and I've got to be at work real early tomorrow morning."

"I won't keep you up. I promise," he said.

"Well, maybe for a little while."

After she and Zionna finished eating dinner, Shenir went through the house quickly straightening up. She purposely did not mention to her daughter that Shane was coming, so she would not be disappointed if he didn't show up.

Shenir looked up at the clock as she ironed a black and white pin-striped skirt for work. *It's already 9 o'clock, if he doesn't get here soon, I'm not letting his butt in the door* she thought.

An hour later, the doorbell rang.

"Hey, baby. You're looking kind of sleepy," said Shane as he entered the house.

"Look, it's really late, Shane. Zionna's already sleep. You really should go—"

Before she completed her sentence, Shane laid a smooth kiss on her mouth, wrapped his arms around her and squeezed her tight. Shenir was taken off guard, and nearly melted in his arms. *My God, it's been so long since he held me*, she thought. Shenir trembled as tears began to stream down her face. She caught herself. Startled, she pushed back. Then he kissed her again and she felt defenseless for her heart still ached for him. They sat on the couch and talked, reminiscing well into the night until Shenir fell asleep in his arms.

THE MORNING AFTER, Zionna entered the living room. "Mommy, Daddy!" she shouted surprised to see them together.

They woke with a start. Shenir looked at the clock on the wooden end table.

"Oh no, it's almost 8:30 Shane! I was supposed to get to work early today. I'm late," Shenir panicked and sat up rubbing her eyes, shaking herself.

"Shenir, slow down. What's the rush, baby—"

"Slow down?" Shenir snapped and shot a look at Shane that could cut glass. "I think I better keep *my* job, since *you're* not here to take care of us!"

"Hey, look. Just say the word and I'm not going anywhere," said Shane.

"You think it's that easy?"

"Well, yes. I do."

Shenir covered her eyes with her hands and wept. She knew she wouldn't make it to downtown Chicago in time for her meeting with her boss Sam.

"I better call and tell them I'm running late."

"Shenir, why don't you just take the day off and let's spend it together, the three of us, like old times, sweetheart."

"That's easy for you to say, seeing that you're off in between construction jobs, Shane!"

"Give it a try, honey. Sam and Regina won't mind. Try, just try," he pleaded. Shane sent Zionna upstairs to go put on her play clothes.

Shenir rolled her eyes and sighed, then picked up the phone and called her job. When the company voicemail system picked up, she left a message. "Julianna, sweetie, can you have Sam call me when he gets in. I have a family matter I have to take care of and I just don't think I can make it in today."

Five minutes later, her boss Sam called.

"Is everything all right, Shenir?" Sam asked, fully aware of her marital issue.

"Yes, Sam. I'm really sorry about this morning. I have a family matter to work out," she explained.

"We all do sometimes, Shenir. Don't worry. I started working on my petition late last night and practically finished it. I'll have Julianna enter a few changes for me," said Sam. "So take care of your business, Shenir, and I'll see you hopefully on tomorrow. All right?"

"Thanks for understanding, Sam." Shenir hung up the phone.

She wiped her brow and settled down on the couch next to Shane. They looked at each other and smiled, relieved that they'd be able to spend the day together as a family for the first time in two weeks. Zionna came back in the living room with her teddy bear, sucking on her thumb and sat on the other side of her father.

"I'm going to school, Mommy?"

"Let's all stay together today and play family again," Shane said to Zionna.

Shenir winced as she heard Shane say *play* family, and Shane noticed. He gave Shenir and Zionna a reassuring hug.

"Hey, Daddy's got the tickle bug," Shane blurted as he grabbed Zionna and tickled her belly. Zionna screamed and giggled with delight.

Shenir prayed silently as she watched her husband and daughter reunite. *Lord Jesus, thank You for bringing Shane home to me. I pray that he will be faithful and that we will be a family for real—not for play. Please help us, oh Lord, and bless us. These things I ask in Your holy name. Amen.*

SHANE AND SHENIR arrived at his mother's house that afternoon after visiting the Lincoln Park Zoo on Chicago's North Side with little Zionna. Their daughter had exhausted herself running down the lanes between the monkey house and the lion's den. She had made faces through the glass at the gorillas and screamed when they hollered back at her. Zionna's light complexion had tanned perfectly in the early fall sun. A pint-sized four-year-old with sandy brown, curly hair, Zionna's smile could light up a room just like her father's smile. "Mommy, Daddy," she yelled earlier that day as she relayed from one parent to the other. Between the three of them, she was the one most excited to be back together as a family. Following a dash in the brisk fall wind, and after leaping into a huge pile of yellow and red fallen leaves, the little bundle of excitement too explosive to imagine, had calmed down and faded gently into a long fall nap during the ride back in her father's Range Rover.

"Hi June," said Shenir as she kissed her mother-in-law on her plump, rosy cheek.

"Shenir, so nice to see you," replied Mama June in her raspy drawl. "Boy, Shaney, why is Zionna knocked out? I wanted to spend a little time with my granddaughter this afternoon."

"Ma, you know she wore us all out at the zoo." Shane laughed and his hazel eyes sparkled.

"But she will probably be out for hours," Mama June poked her lips out and then shrugged her shoulders in disappointment. "I haven't seen Zionna in nearly a month. Why don't you wake her up, Shaney."

"Zionna was so sleepy, June. She really needs her rest," said Shenir.

"Shenir, I'm not even going to argue with you," said Mama June. "Although, I'm sure she would be okay if we wake her up." She looked at her son and raised her eyebrows.

"I'll just wake her up for now," said Shane as he reached over Shenir and grabbed Zionna's leg and shook it.

Shenir rolled her eyes upward and let out an irritated sigh. *June always gets her way*, she thought. Mama June grinned victoriously as Zionna arose and yawned with a grumpy expression and began to cry.

"Oh precious, come give grandma a hug," she drew Zionna close to her bosom and gave her a squeeze. Zionna rubbed her eyes and smiled shyly, covering her face with her hands.

"You hungry, baby?" Mama June asked, but Zionna shook her head no. "Shenir, why don't you go and fix a plate for Zionna. I've got some Spaghetti O's in the cabinet."

"Oh, we're not staying that long, June," said Shenir.

Shane shot an angry look at Shenir. "I'll do it," said Shane as he arose and went to the kitchen.

"So, you and my son back together?" June asked while Shane was out of the room.

"We're working things out slowly."

"Shenir, a career girl like you should just let go and get on with your life."

"Excuse me?" Shenir couldn't believe her ears.

"Shaney has really been going through a lot, missing his daughter and all."

"Shane was the one who cheated, and I am the one who has been through a lot!"

"Shaney could certainly do a lot better. You're obviously not his type. Pastor Houghton and I could take Shaney and Zionna in and help him raise the girl."

"How dare you!"

"Just a suggestion," Mama June stopped speaking as Shane entered the room.

Zionna had fallen back to sleep in Mama June's lap.

"Shane, I have a headache, let's just go please," Shenir said as she picked up Zionna and took her to the Range Rover.

"What happened, Ma?" asked Shane.

"Shenir's upset that's all. I guess it's just too much for her emotionally for the three of you to be back together so soon. Take her home, Shaney. I'll be okay."

He gave his mother a kiss and left out.

THE RIDE HOME WAS SILENT as Shane drove. Shenir chose silence over trying to tell Shane about his mother. *He is such a mama's boy he won't believe a word I say. June has never been supportive of our relationship nor our marriage. Five years of June's snide remarks whenever Shane is out of earshot is what it is—but she really went too far suggesting taking Zionna.* Shenir trembled at the thought of losing her daughter. She had seen such cases in her career as a legal assistant but never imagined it could be her life. She closed her eyes and drifted into a restless sleep.

LOVER'S QUARREL

"And I will betroth thee unto Me forever; yea, I will betroth thee to Me in righteousnesss, and in judgment, and in lovingkindness, and in mercies. I will even betroth thee unto Me in faithfulness: and thou shalt know the LORD."
— Hosea 2:19-20 (KJV)

Let's kiss and make up. In romantic tales, the valiant and handsome man always ends up embracing his love and sealing their relationship with a kiss—no matter what they have endured. Love will keep them together.

God is love. He is our romantic King of kings who has rescued our souls from the pit of hell. No matter what we have gone through together, He forgives us. As long as we are willing to confess our sins and repent, we can kiss and make up.

Chapter 4

Bottom Line

SHENIR SANG THE AL GREEN SONG, "Let's Stay Together" as it resounded from WWJD, the dusty radio station. She was preparing a meal fit for a king—after all her king was home again. It had been almost two weeks since that Monday night Shane dropped in and lit her fire. And she was feeling like her old loving self again.

It was Saturday night, and she was frying a skillet full of Cajun spiced catfish to go with the pot of collard greens, candied yams and cornbread muffins she'd prepared earlier that evening. Shenir was making Shane's favorite meal because everyone knows that the way to a man's heart is through his stomach. She wanted to try to talk her husband into going to church with her and Zionna the next morning. Shane hardly ever went to church with her before they broke up. Shenir was convinced that his relationship with the Lord—or lack thereof—was the main reason why he was tempted to cheat on her in the first place. Even though Shane was a PK—preacher's kid—he was spiritually disconnected. She also knew that the church he grew up in was more "religious" than "spiritual" and that Shane endured religious practices and traditions growing up rather than enjoying an intimate relationship with the Lord. She thought about how he always brushed her off whenever she would invite him. It had become so routine for him to say, "Y'all go ahead without me. I'm not into all that shouting and stuff." So she just stopped asking him altogether, which was fine with him because he'd sit around all day Sunday flipping through the sports channels and drinking beer. But now, she was determined to make his relationship with the Lord a condition of their marriage. *This time*, she thought, *we're going to make it—but the Lord has got to be the center of our life.*

Shane entered the kitchen, stretching and yawning from a long nap. He grabbed a piece of catfish that Shenir had just removed from the skillet.

"Ummm, this is good, honey. I see you haven't lost your touch girl," Shane said as he munched on the fish.

"There's lots I haven't lost, Mr. Houghton."

"Uh oh, so it's *Mr. Houghton*. What have I done now?"

"You haven't done anything. I've just been meaning to talk with you about something," Shenir began. "I was wondering if you would come to church with me and Zionna tomorrow?"

"Oh, baby, you know how I feel about that shouting and screaming and stuff. Besides, I planned to watch the football game tomorrow with Brian and James at their cousin Tom's house. Why don't y'all just go without me this time," he said.

"That's it, Shane! I've had it up to here! That's why we fell apart the first time. You let the devil trick you into sinning, and you know it's time for you to turn your life over to the Lord. Don't you think it's time Shane?"

"Shenir, I know who the Lord is and I don't have to go to church to find out. So why don't you lay off."

"But Shane," Shenir overflowed with emotion. "You've got to receive Jesus as your Lord and Savior. Don't you get it yet? Or do we have to go through hell all over again before you realize you've got the enemy trying to influence you?"

"Honey, the mistake I made was all on my own. I accepted the blame and I apologized. Now you got to play all holy. Can't we just get on with our lives?" he said.

"I really don't know if we can make it, Shane. We need the Lord in our lives—both of us. He is the only One who can keep us from falling. I don't want to take any more chances with our marriage. Why can't you be with your family on Sunday at church? Come to the Lord's house on Sunday Shane."

"Look, okay, if it means that much to you, I'll go—but just this once. I have other things to do on Sunday, you know."

"No, I don't know. I mean, what in the world could be more important to you than God?" Shenir shook her head and left the kitchen.

THE NEXT MORNING, Shenir was up bright and early ironing everyone's clothes for church. She put in a Gospel CD with all the latest hits and turned up the sound system.

"Do you have to play that music so loud, baby?" Shane yelled as he entered the kitchen where she was ironing. "What's for breakfast?"

"I made some waffles and sausage. Sit down and I'll fix your plate," she said as she forked over a few sausages and poured syrup over a stack of waffles.

"Honey, about church. You know, maybe you two should just go without me—"

"Look, Mr. Houghton," Shenir started waving a fork as she spoke, "you said you would go with me today and I'm not taking no, nevermind, go without me, or anything else for an answer. Okay, dear?"

"Fine. Where's my shirt?" Shane got up from the table without touching his food and grabbed his shirt off the ironing board. He stormed off into the bathroom and turned on the shower.

"Thank you, Jesus!" Shenir said softly as she lifted her hands in praise.

THEY ARRIVED AT THE CHURCH, Shane carrying Zionna in his left arm and holding Shenir's hand with his right. Although they got there a few minutes late, Shenir was simply glad that they'd made it—together, as a family—the Houghtons on one accord with the Lord. They went and sat in the main sanctuary, already crowded with people shouting and giving honor to the Lord Jesus Christ. The praise dancers moved as graceful as ballerinas as they entered the room waving white banners in sweet surrender to the Lord, some leaping with gold streamers spiraling to exalt His royalty.

As the church clapped and sang, Shane's eye was captured by a woman sitting in the pews on the right side of the sanctuary. Then he recognized her—it was Vanessa, Shenir's friend with whom Shane had an affair. Vanessa noticed Shane watching her and smiled. Then Shane smiled back at her and motioned with his eyes for her to come out in the lobby.

"Honey, I've got to go to the men's room. I'll be right back," he told Shenir.

Shenir had missed the glances between Shane and Vanessa as she was immersed in worship. She moved her knees as he walked past her through the pews. But that's when she saw Vanessa get up and make her way to the exit. Shenir took Shane's hand before he cleared the pew, and got up with him.

"I think I'd better go as well," Shenir said. "Will you keep an eye on Zi for me?" she asked her neighbor Sister Hattie Mae, who was like a second grandmother to Zionna.

"Gone girl, you know Zi's fine with me." Zionna remained in the pew, seated next to Sister Hattie Mae.

When they reached the lobby, Vanessa was standing in front of the glass wall of "The Secret Place," the church bookstore down the hallway. Gazing at her reflection, Vanessa pulled out a makeup sponge and wiped the tiny beads of perspiration from her chocolate brown skin that were building on her forehead and nose. She smoothed out her black velvet dress and applied a fresh coat of cherry red lipstick to match the fiery red hair weave she had just gotten done a day ago.

"Good morning, Vanessa," Shenir said icely as she stepped up to her.

Unable to look Shenir in the eye, Vanessa returned the greeting with a nod. Shane kept walking by as though he didn't even see Vanessa and entered the men's room.

"Hello, Shenir," Vanessa nearly whispered.

"You looking for a new book? There's one that I think you'd like, *How To Find Love In The Lord: A Single Woman's Guide*. Don't you think it's time you stopped trying to hook up with *my* man?" Shenir said indignantly.

"Shenir, I've changed."

"If that's true, why were you coming out here to meet my husband?"

"Look, I *was* coming out here to meet him, but it was not for what you think. I was going to tell him that I'm a different woman. I really have changed, Shenir."

"Yes, I can tell by how every curve is showing in your dress—out here putting on lipstick and fixing yourself up. Who are you trying to fool?" Shenir rolled her eyes at Vanessa and folded her arms in disgust.

Vanessa broke down in tears. "Shenir, I'm really sorry. You've got it *all*—I just want to be blessed too. I'm not the same, honest, I'm not. Please believe me," she pleaded. She reached out to touch Shenir's shoulder but Shenir jerked away. Vanessa bowed her head and walked away, re-entering the main sanctuary.

As Shane came out of the men's room, Shenir confronted him.

"Shane, what a coincidence that Vanessa would be out here in the lobby as you came out isn't it?"

"Shenir, it's not what it looks like."

"Yeah, baby, I know," Shenir said in a curt whisper. "We'll deal with this later." She let the matter go for the moment, and they went back to their seats in the sanctuary.

Shenir knelt down and prayed. "Oh, Lord, I can't take this again. Please Heavenly Father, bless my house and renew in me a right spirit that can handle what's ahead. I fear that my husband isn't finished playing games. Lord, please change his heart and make him a faithful husband. In Jesus' Name I pray. Amen."

Shane overheard her prayer, not that she was trying to be real discreet. He tried to play it off. A little embarrassed, Shane bowed his head and covered his face with his hands.

Pastor Michael Huddle came up to the pulpit and blessed the congregation, then he began.

"There was a thirsty woman, not from the best part of town. Every day she would go to the same place at the same time to quench her thirst—until the day she met Jesus, that's when her thirst was fulfilled.

"Today, this woman might be a prostitute on the street corner, or a crackhead in an abandoned building, or maybe the 'other' woman longing for a husband. Nevertheless, she is thirsty—she wants money, her next hit of drugs, or she's thirsty for love in all the wrong places.

"In John 4:4-26, it was the Samaritan Woman, filling her water pot. Every day, at the same time, at the same place. But this was the day that Jesus showed up. He knew that she'd be there! After all, He is God in the flesh—there's nothing He doesn't know about you! He knew her thirst exceeded her resources. She'd had five husbands and was working on number six. But she was about to meet blessed number seven, her Heavenly Bridegroom, the One And Only.

"Anyone know what I'm talking about?"

Shenir looked at Vanessa until she caught her eye and then Shenir shook her head and muttered under her breath,

"Yeah, you thirsty. You want my man and God knows who else's." Vanessa turned her attention back to the preacher and then bowed her head in prayer.

LATER THAT EVENING after Shenir washed and put away the dinner dishes, she went into the washroom and ran warm water in the tub for a bath. She went into her bedroom and removed her clothes, putting on her favorite fluffy white terrycloth robe. As she stood in front of her dresser mirror, she let her long black wavy hair down her back and began to brush it. Just then Shane entered the bedroom. Shenir tried to ignore him, still upset from the scene at church that morning. He walked up behind her and put his arms around her waist, kissing her softly on her neck.

"Shane, stop," she said as she jerked away from him.

She stormed out the bedroom and went into the bathroom. He raced after her, but she slammed the bathroom door in his face and locked the door.

"Shenir, why are you trippin'?" he demanded in a disgusted tone.

"Why don't you just let me have some space," she yelled back as she hung up her robe and stepped into the hot bath.

"Fine, if that's the way you want it. I'm out of here," said Shane. Then he grabbed his jacket and got his keys off the dresser and left out the front door.

Shenir heard him slam the door as he walked out. "He ain't no good," she said angrily, "Why do I even put up with that trifling man?"

She laid back in the warm sudsy bubbles. As the heat of the bath began to soothe her tense body, she closed her eyes. A strange vision came across her mind. *Shenir was standing at the altar at church, dressed in a glorious flowing wedding gown with a train that flowed nearly ten feet behind her. She was holding a bouquet of twelve dead roses. Suddenly the groom appeared wearing a red crushed velvet late 1970s retro-style tuxedo, but the groom was not Shane. Instead, He was a tall, handsome Middle Eastern foreigner with an olive complexion and raven black curly hair. His doe-like eyes were honey brown with an intensity unlike any she had ever seen. He was wearing a golden crown and His warm, inviting smile could melt an iceburg. "I've been waiting for you, My love," He said. He extended his hand and touched her dead flowers and all twelve roses came back to life.*

Shenir was awakened from her vision by the sound of loud knocking on the front door. She jumped out the tub, nearly slipping on the wet bathroom linoleum floor. She put her robe on and looked through the peep hole of the front door. It was Shane, cursing and very drunk. She was afraid to open the door.

"Shenir! Open the door!" he yelled as he banged on the door. He kept it up for about 15 minutes, hollering and screaming profanities at the top of his lungs. Then he stopped. A few more minutes passed, then all of a sudden he kicked the door in, ripping it off of the hinges.

"Shane!" Shenir screamed in a state of shock.

"I lost my keys and you couldn't even open the door!" Shane yelled, "Who do you think you are some kind of *queen*?!"

He ran up to her and slapped her hard across the face, knocking her to the floor. Shenir crawled toward the telephone, and Shane began kicking her. Shenir cried out for him to stop.

Zionna came down the stairs screaming "Mommy! Daddy! Stop!"

Just as Shane turned to look at Zionna, Shenir managed to get to her feet and grabbed her daughter. She ran out the front door, crossing the lawn to the next door neighbor's house.

"Let me in! Please help me!" Shenir cried. The neighbor's front porch light came on and the door opened just before Shane reached the bottom of the porch stairs.

"Oh, my God!" said the neighbor, Mrs. Stuart, as she saw the blood trickling off the side of Shenir's face. Then Mrs. Stuart called out to her husband, "Harvey, call the police!" Shenir entered the front door and Harvey Stuart came to the door to block Shane from entering. Shane wrestled with Mr. Stuart, but the six-foot tall, husky 48-year-old fireman threw Shane back and shut the door. About five minutes later, the police pulled up in a squad car and wrestled Shane to the ground, pinning him face down before handcuffing him. After they read him his rights, they seated him in the back of the police car. An ambulance arrived as the police were questioning Mr. Stuart. Mrs. Stuart kept watch over Zionna, who was crying and trembling, as Shenir got into the ambulance and rode to the hospital. Police met up with her at the hospital to take her statement. At the police station, Shane was booked for assault and battery and disorderly conduct.

Shenir had sustained bruises on her forehead, back and abdominal area. As she laid in the emergency room bed pending release that same night, she wept as she tried to make up her mind about whether she would press charges against her husband.

Her sister Mimi arrived at the hospital about thirty minutes later.

"Uh-uh, girl, no he didn't," said Mimi as she touched the side of Shenir's face. Shenir winced from pain as her sister lifted her chin to get a better look, "I'm going to kill Shane! What the devil got into him?"

As they sat in the hospital room, Shenir filled Mimi in on the events of the day, how Shane had tried to slip off to see Vanessa in church, that he stormed out when she played him off later that evening, and how he came back drunk and kicked the front door in then proceeded to kick and beat her.

"Shenir, you've got to press charges. You can't let him get away with all this. What if he had of hit Zionna, then what? They need to lock him up and throw away the key!"

"Mimi, you can't tell Mamasita right now, okay? Let me tell her when I'm ready. I'm just not ready to deal with the family getting all involved. I've got to deal with this on my own."

"Shenir, now is when you need family the most. Besides, we need to make some calls to deal with Shane—how about cousin Roberto? You know he ain't going for this!"

"No, Mimi. That's just what I mean. Look, even though this happened, Shane is still my family—he's Zionna's father."

"God is Zionna's Father—Shane is something from out of space!" retorted Mimi. "So, how are you going to explain your face to Zionna? You going to tell her Daddy had to give you a whipping because you was a bad girl?"

Shenir broke down in tears, and Mimi held her.

The arresting officer approached them.

"Mrs. Houghton, we can hold him for 24 hours, but after that he's free to go, unless you press charges," said Officer Jones.

"What *should* I do?" Shenir asked, not really wanting an answer.

The officer shot her a frustrated look, shook his head in disbelief and walked away.

"I can't, Mimi, I just can't. I'm too shook up right now to deal with this. Take me home, just take me back home."

As they rode back to Shenir's house in silence, Shenir prayed softly and a gentle rain began to fall. *Lord Jesus, You are sovereign and Your Name is above all names. I seek Your help. Lord, what should I do? I can't even think straight now. Please help me deal with this man. How can I just forgive and forget when he has raised his hand against me? How can I even think about taking him back? I just can't handle this—it's too great a problem for me to deal with. Lord, please take over. Please make everything all right again...*

Mimi turned on the windshield wipers and hit the radio buttons until she reached a song she liked. She hummed to the tune of "Congratulations," by Vesta. As the singer bellowed out her melancholy melody, Shenir recalled her late night vision, wondering if the alluring Prince in her dream was the Lord Jesus Himself coming to whisk her away from her tragic life. *I wish I could escape with Him*, she thought.

LET'S ESCAPE

"He that dwelleth in the secret place of the most High shall abide under the shadow of the Almighty...Because he hath set his love upon Me, therefore will I deliver him: I will set him on high, because he hath known My name."
— **Psalm 91:1, 14 (KJV)**

When it is time to break away from all that troubles us, we who love the Lord have a place of comfort: in the arms of our Maker, our Heavenly Husband, who loves us dearly and longs to deliver us and hide us in His bosom.

Loving the Lord and knowing the precious name of Jesus that is above all names, is the key to your escape. It is His secret place on high away from all the madness of the world, where we find our Deliverer. His arms are open to receive us, comfort us and protect us. You can even find this place during good times of your life if you take the time to "be still" and "know that He is God." Just close your eyes, pray, make melody in your heart unto Him, worship your King and delight in the Lord Jesus Christ. And He will manifest His secret place to you.

Chapter 5

A Time For Love

SHENIR TOOK THE WEEK OFF from work to recuperate from the events of the weekend. Her mother stayed with her and slept with Zionna, helped to cook meals and kept the house in order while Shenir got some rest. A retired nurse and church mother, Mrs. Sweet "Mamasita" Sanchez was a loving caregiver and a God-fearing Christian.

"Holy, holy, holy, Lord God Almighty. Worthy is the Lamb of God, Jesus! Hallelujah! I love you Jesus!" Mamasita shouted as she walked through Shenir's house giving praise to the Lord and binding evil spirits, casting them into dry places. As she prayed her way through the hall, she stopped to admire a portrait of Jesus laying on the hall table that Zionna had colored from a Christian coloring book which Mamasita intended to put up on the wall. It was a Sunday School project she had completed the morning before that horrible night when Shane attacked Shenir. Zionna had given the coloring to her grandmother right before the worship service began.

"Nana look what I drew!" said Zionna, grinning from ear to ear. "It's Jesus!"

"Oh, baby, that's so precious! I'm going to frame it and then your Mommy can lift up the Lord in her house! What do you think?"

"Yes, Nana, that's what I want to do—lift up Jesus high, so He can look over Mommy and Daddy," said Zionna.

"We'll surprise them, huh? And, I'll take it with me and bring it back in a beautiful frame when I come by on Wednesday after Bible study," she told her granddaughter.

When she'd arrived that Monday morning to "keep watch," Mamasita brought the portrait with her in a golden metal frame. As Mamasita reflected on their secret exchange, she wondered if she simply should have let Zionna bring the portrait straight home—perhaps the portrait of Jesus would have reminded Shane to keep his hands off her daughter. She wasted no time in taking Shane's portrait off the wall and replacing it with the portrait of Jesus. Silently, as she placed the picture on the wall, she prayed, *Lord Jesus, while this is a lovely drawing designed by the hands of Your sweet child Zionna, still You are truly more beautiful than any of us could ever imagine—more beautiful than the children of men! I place this coloring here to remind everyone in this household that you are ever present and watchful over us. Bless this house oh Lord, set a watch over every soul that enters in and out, embracing everyone with Your love, covering each visitor with Your precious Blood. Thank You, Lord Jesus! Amen.*

Mamasita believed in blessing a house right out of a storm! Now it was afternoon, and as she gazed at the portrait on the wall—a golden-complexioned vision of the Lord with curly black hair, honey brown doe-like eyes and a smile as bright as the sun—she sang a Bible passage from the Song of Solomon (5:10-16):

My beloved is white and ruddy, the chiefest among ten thousand.

His head is as the most fine gold, His locks are bushy and black as a raven.

His eyes are as the eyes of doves by the rivers of waters, washed with milk, and fitly set.

His cheeks are as a bed of spices, as sweet flowers; his lips like lilies, dropping sweet smelling myrrh.

His hands are as gold rings set with the beryl: His belly is as bright ivory overlaid with sapphires.

His legs are as pillars of marble, set upon sockets of fine gold: His countenance is as Lebanon, excellent as the cedars.

His mouth is most sweet: yea, He is altogether lovely.

This is my beloved, and this is my friend, O daughters of Jerusalem.

Shenir was walking down the stairs following a long nap, when she heard her mother singing. She smiled as she remembered how Mamasita tucked her in at night with that same sweet love song. Her heart was comforted and filled with a joy that took away the sorrow tugging at her emotions.

"Mamasita, where does that song come from?"

"Oh honey, you mean you've never read the *Song Of Solomon* in the *Holy Bible*?"

"Well, not really, Mamasita. I've been studying the New Testament, and have read some of the Old Testament, but I don't remember reading those words," confessed Shenir.

She sat down with her mother and they opened the large white family Bible that Shenir had on the mantle of the fireplace in her living room. As Mamasita turned the gold-coated pages, she continued to hum softly.

"Darling, you must learn the identity of your True Love. No man can ever take His place. No man can ever fulfill your needs the way Jesus can. Trust Him and He will bring you through this break up. Sometimes He must allow the breaking up of the fallow ground of your heart," said Mamasita. "But that's only so He can have room to come in.

And right now, He wants to fill every area of your heart with His love, True Love."

Shenir listened to her mother as she began to minister in song.

"Sing to Him, honey. Tell Him about your aching heart. Pretty soon your heart will only ache for His love, and He will not break your heart that you dedicate to Him," urged Mamasita. Soon they were both singing sweet melodies to the Lord.

"Do you have a nice gospel CD you can play?" asked Mamasita.

"Well, I've got a really nice worship CD by CeCe Winans entitled *Alone In His Presence*," answered Shenir.

"That sounds really nice. Why don't you play that while we read?" instructed Mamasita.

Together that afternoon, they read the entire book of the *Song Of Solomon* as the melodies of worship and praise played softly in the background. Shenir and Mamasita took turns reading the loving verses.

"Let Him kiss me with the kisses of His mouth: for thy love is better than wine, (1:2)" Shenir began softly.

Mamasita gently blew a love kiss in the air and waved her hand to offer her affection to the Lord. Then she walked slowly around the living room. As Shenir completed the first three verses of the first chapter, Mamasita began with verse 4.

"Draw me, we will run after Thee: the King hath brought me into His chambers: we will be glad and rejoice in Thee, we will remember thy love more than wine: the upright love thee."

As Mamasita read, Shenir closed her eyes and swayed in her seat on the tan leather sofa. CeCe Winans' melodic voice serenaded the Lord in the background, as the title track played, "Alone In His Presence."

When I'm alone with you, my soul learns worship, in spirit and in truth...

The sweet melody helped bring Shenir closer to the Lord. A vision of Jesus asking His disciples to remember Him as He poured wine and broke bread came to her mind. "I will remember You more than wine my Lord," Shenir spoke lovingly to Jesus as though just the two of them were in the room for she had escaped to the Secret Place of her heart. The joy of the Lord filled her up. When Shenir read the fourth verse in Chapter 3, tears began to trickle down her cheeks.

"It was but a little that I passed from them, but I found Him whom my soul loveth. I held Him, and would not let Him go..."

Shenir fell to her knees upon the floor and wept. She raised both her hands and called out, "Jesus! Jesus! Jesus!"

Shenir began to shout and her spirit was renewed. A sweet floral aroma filled the room as they sang. It was unlike any experience Shenir ever had in her life. That day her fire was lit for the Lord as He rekindled her desire to get to know Him, a desire that she had as a child but now as a woman she began to embrace. Jesus was her Heavenly Husband, her Beloved Bridegroom.

PASTOR KEN HOUGHTON WAS NOT accustomed to visiting inmates in jail. He had never taken the time to set up outreach programs in his storefront church, Solid Rock Christian Church. His congregation of about 25 was slowly dwindling each month. One lady even told him before she left, "Pastor Houghton, there is just no spirit in this church. All you all do is go through the motions." That statement struck him as insulting for he felt that he had run a tight ship. Services were held on Sunday at 9:30 a.m. for Sunday School, 11:00 a.m. for Worship, and Wednesday at 7:00 p.m. for Bible Study. On Sunday there was one hour of Sunday School, a half hour continental breakfast break, and service promptly began at 11:00 a.m. The two deacons, Thomas Stowdy and Robert Press, would begin singing "Pray For

Me." The church would sing a hymn from the hymnal book, be seated for announcements, then he would give his sermon, do an alter call and release the church with a benediction. Every moment was perfectly timed, and it was all over by 12:30 p.m. Every now and then during announcements someone would attempt to interrupt service with a testimony, but he did not allow such disturbances in the church program. He used to have Shane occasionally give the benediction, but that son of his stopped showing up when he graduated from high school.

Look at Shane now, Pastor Houghton thought. *Got to speak to him through this glass window.*

"Hi Pops," Shane greeted his father.

"Hi young man," Pastor Houghton cleared his throat. "I was going to post your bond today. Your mother thought that it would be in your best interest for you to stay with us."

"How is Shenir and Zionna?" Shane rubbed the scratch above his eye made by Shenir when she was trying to defend herself against him.

"Shenir has a restraining order against you and is pressing charges."

"What? She didn't have to do that! How am I going to see my daughter?"

"Look Shane, you need to focus on getting yourself together. You've got to stop drinking and fooling around," said Pastor Houghton. "Shenir doesn't even know about all these different women you've been bringing into my home while you were staying with us during your breakup."

"Pops, look, I'm a grown man."

"Not behind these bars you're not! You're nothing but a criminal to me. You are a real loser. How could you beat up on that pretty wife of yours?"

"She had it coming—and so do you!"

"Shame on you!" said Pastor Houghton. "I'm not posting your bond."

"But, Pops—come on—I—"

"You what? You're not my *real* son anyway!"

Shane bowed his head. Then he scooted his chair back and got up, walking away from the window. He called for the guard and left his father stewing in anger.

LATER THAT AFTERNOON the guard called Shane Houghton's name for lunch. There was no answer. The other inmates were hooping and hollering. "Ooooh Shane, can you come out and play?" yelled one inmate.

The jail guard entered the row, rattling the bars with his billy-club as he walked to Shane's cell. He took his keys from the ring on his belt and prepared to open the cell.

"Oh God," said the guard.

There was Shane hanging from the bars by his ripped t-shirt. He was dead.

FIVE DAYS LATER Shane's body was laid at the altar in an open casket at Solid Rock Christian Church. Pastor Ken Houghton and First Lady June Houghton were seated up in the front row. It was the one time that Mama June ever wore black in her lifetime.

Shenir entered the sanctuary wearing a black skirt suit and black velvet hat with a lace veil. She slowly walked over to Shane's parents to pay her respects. Mama June's light-skinned complexion was beet red and her eyes were swollen nearly shut. She arose from her seat and looked Shenir directly in the eye, gritted her teeth and stonely spoke.

"You killed him. You killed my Shaney." Mama June's face twitched and her body started to tremble.

Pastor Houghton put his arms around his wife and sat her down. He took a handkerchief from his pocket and gently wiped her face. He sat there holding her securely for the remainder of the service.

Shortly after that, Dirksen arrived and greeted the Houghtons. Then he went over to Shenir and sat next to her for a moment to offer his condolences.

"Hi Shenir, how are you holding up," Dirksen put his hands on her shoulders and tried to make eye contact with her. She began to weep.

"I can't believe he's gone," tears ran down Shenir's face into her mouth. Mimi, who was seated on the opposite side of her sister, passed a tissue to her. Shenir took the tissue and softly wiped her face and blew her nose. "Zionna won't have a father. It's so sad right now. I know Shane and I broke up but I just can't believe Shane left us like this, not this way. He didn't have to take his own life."

"Shenir, God will care for you. Don't be afraid. He will always be there," said Dirksen.

Shenir nodded but she could no longer hold it together and began to wail. Dirksen embraced her and Mimi handed him another tissue. He dried Shenir's eyes and promised her she could call on him for support.

"Shenir, if you need anything—anything at all, please call me," Dirksen kissed her on her forehead, got up, and proceeded to the pulpit to start the formal prayer to begin the funeral service for his late friend Shane.

APPLE OF HIS EYE

"Therefore, if any man be in Christ, he is a new creature: old things are passed away; behold, all things are become new."
— II Corinthians 5:17 (KJV)

God is in love with His bride, His church, His people. As believers, we are the apple of His eye. He is constantly fussing over us, primping and priming us for His pleasure. His heart is smitten. He perfects us with His love. The moment you say to Him, I do, you become His and He transforms you into a new creature of beauty.

A Sweet 16 coming of age story takes place in Ezekiel Chapter 16:8-14, the moment the LORD lays eyes on Jerusalem. Before our eyes, a lost one becomes a loved one as the LORD passes by His lady love and claims her for Himself, cleanses her of her sin, anoints her, dresses her in fine linen and adorns her with precious jewels. And, as a final touch, He crowns her with His beauty, so that she is perfect in the sight of all mankind. Yes, that's what it's like to be loved by the Master, to be transformed into His treasure.

Chapter 6

Let's Walk Together

"**D**O YOU TRUST ME?" asked Mimi, as she sat in the kitchen of Shenir's home snapping string beans to freeze for the fast approaching Thanksgiving holiday.

"Yes, but I just don't think I'm ready for a date yet," Shenir voiced with strong conviction. "My heart is not completely healed, and you're trying to set me up with someone I know absolutely nothing about."

"You've got to jump back in the water sooner or later girl. Don't you think you deserve a better life, Shenir?"

"I do, but I just don't think it's time to look for a replacement. Okay?"

It was nearly the end of November, and it had been just over a month and a half since Shane died. But instead of wallowing in sorrow, Shenir chose to leave her burdens at the altar and energized her life in the Lord. She began getting involved with the Mall Missions Ministry of her church, hosting worship services in the local malls featuring her church choir and witnessing in the halls of the malls in groups.

"Shenir, you've got too much going for you to just allow yourself to go to waste," said Mimi, "I know you need a man!"

"Mimi, I've got a man—and I'm not talking about an earthly man. My man is sweet, pure and holy—all that and more. In fact, Jesus is more than enough man for me—He's my Lord. He's my focus," said Shenir with a joyful look on her face.

"Wow, Shenir, you make it sound like you and Jesus got a good thing going on!" Mimi laughed to the point of tears.

"You see, Mimi, that's where you and I are different. I've just grown closer to Him, and He's shown me a thing or two about true love. He doesn't lie to me. He doesn't cheat on me. He doesn't beat me up," Shenir said with a slight sigh. "You've got to understand, these past few months, Jesus has pulled me through, girl. I mean really."

"Well, I don't know. I know what Mamasita has taught me. But you're still human, Shenir. I mean, don't you think Jesus would want you to go on with your life?" asked Mimi.

"Jesus is my life," Shenir responded. "And we're going on with our life just fine."

As Shenir began to reflect on the month she had been spending walking with her Savior, a sense of pure satisfaction rushed over her. She knew that she had not wasted a minute of her life. What's more, she felt empowered. All of the issues concerning her failed marriage and widowhood were simply placed into the arms of her Savior. She didn't think that she was in denial. She just felt like she had found the answer to all of life's problems in Jesus. Shenir was starting to get irritated by her sister's insistence on her getting a man—after all God is love and she was getting plenty of love from the Lord.

"Shenir, you're getting a little carried away—don't you think?"

"As a matter of fact, Mimi, I am. I'm carried away with Christ and I trust Him completely to direct my life," answered Shenir. "One day—and I hope it doesn't take something like what happened between me and Shane to make you wake up—you will realize that the Lord is all you truly need."

"Girl, I know I need the Lord. But I mean, come on now. I've got to get my groove on!" Mimi laughed.

"When He calls you, Mimi, you will answer," said Shenir.

"Shenir, you scare me when you talk like that!"

Shenir smiled and walked away, leaving Mimi in the kitchen to ponder their conversation.

Mimi sat down at the table and continued to snap string beans. She wondered when her sister was going to come around to her way of seeing things. It seemed like Shenir had changed dramatically since her life with Shane ended. Mimi understood her sister's need for the Lord, but why was she going overboard? As she snapped a bean, she pondered some more. Finally, it dawned on her that maybe there might be something to all this talking and walking in the Lord that her sister was doing. After all, Shenir was doing pretty good for herself. She was paying all her bills even though she no longer had the support of her late husband. Shenir had gotten a raise *and* a promotion on her job from legal secretary to office manager. Sister girl just traded in her red sedan for a bronze luxury car. She was meeting her mortgage payments, even three months ahead. Mimi, considered all of the good that had come to Shenir even after all that drama with Shane, and she realized it was true. The Lord is some kind of Lover.

"Shenir!" called Mimi.

"What is it Mimi?"

"When is the next worship service at The Plaza?" asked Mimi.

"Oh, that one's going to be this Friday. Why, do you want to come?"

"I think I might check it out."

"Be on time then—it starts at 7 p.m. And dress casual, wear your jeans—because it's not about what you wear, it's about what's going on in the inside, Ms. Thing."

Mimi thought about what she should wear, but then began to think about all the men she could meet. That's when she thought, maybe she could dress up some. Well, she had two days to think about it.

"Oh, and Mimi?"

"Yes, Shenir?"

"Don't come in looking for Mr. Right. After all, He's already in your heart."

Mimi grinned because her sister had her number. She snapped a few more green beans and threw them in a bowl of water.

"Now, what makes you think I'm only out to catch?"

"I know you Mimi!" Shenir laughed.

ON FRIDAY NIGHT Mimi arrived at The Plaza early at about six o'clock. She hung out at Chaka's Boutique on the second floor, hiding out behind the hats and checking out the latest styles—and watching the men as they walked down the hall.

"Can I help you with anything?" asked the clerk, who was wearing a strange purple and orange hat shaped like a rose with antennae sticking out of it.

"I'm just looking," said Mimi as she picked up a red knit beret that read: "Kiss Me All Over."

"Now, that's you!" exclaimed the clerk. "Try it on. I think it would look lovely over your curls."

Mimi grinned and the clerk began to finger comb Mimi's short curly black locks, guiding each ringlet behind her ears as she positioned the beret upon Mimi's head. The clerk tilted the hat from side to side, finally setting the hat straight.

"I particularly like this number because it brings out a woman's facial features, like your dimples. There's no brim to hide behind, so you get the full effect of that bright beautiful smile of yours and those gorgeous green eyes," the salesperson lavished, not realizing Mimi was wearing color contact lenses over her light brown eyes.

"Well, I don't know. I mean, I think it makes my head look a little too big," said Mimi as she gazed at her reflection in the mirror.

"Nonsense! You have a beautiful forehead. Not like some of the women I've seen, my goodness, you think they're mama's grew them from a watermelon patch!"

Mimi and the clerk fell out laughing.

"What's your name?" asked Mimi.

"Delilah," answered the clerk.

"You just made my day. Delilah, I think I'll rock this cap," said Mimi.

"You do that girl! And what's *your* name?"

"Mimi."

"Now you know this hat has Mimi written all over it!"

"Well, I like that it says 'Kiss Me All Over'!"

"I'm sure that special man will when you wear it," chimed Delilah.

Mimi left the boutique wearing her new red beret, which complemented her already jazzy denim skirt suit and black leather high-heeled boots. It was a quarter to seven and she was ready for Mr. Right. She was led by the sound of guitars and keyboard notes cueing up for the evening. As she made her way to the sound stage, she could see Shenir. Then she stopped dead in her tracks as she saw the most handsome man she'd ever laid eyes on seated behind the keyboard. He had smooth cocoa brown skin. And his hair was cut close and wavy, faded around the edges. His almond-shaped eyes sparkled in a soulful brown color that could melt any woman's heart. She could see that his body was solid as she peeped his muscular arms with each stroke of the keyboard. *Now,* she thought, *I'm in heaven.*

"Mimi!" shouted Shenir from the other side of the sound stage as she ran to hug her sister. The keyboardist took notice of Mimi as she met her sister halfway. "Let me introduce you to everyone."

They walked over to the musician stand and Shenir introduced her to the band members.

"Hey 'yall, this is my sister, Mimi," Shenir said proudly. "Mimi, this is Jovanni our keyboardist and girl he can really play!"

My goodness he's fine, thought Mimi. As Shenir introduced Mimi to the rest of the group, Mimi hardly paid attention because her focus was on Jovanni.

At seven o'clock, the keyboardist began to play a soft melody while singing the words,

I'm dedicated to Him.
He's shown me favor and lit a fire within me.
I'm changed forever more.
He's worked a miracle in me.
Changed. Dedicated. Changed. Dedicated. Changed. Dedicated.
I'm dedicated to Him.

Mimi swayed to Jovanni's voice. His vocals were a perfect blend of Brian McKnight, Luther Vandross and heaven on earth, if you could imagine such a sound! Her thoughts were centered on Jovanni. She began to wonder what he was like before he got saved, as if he even needed to change. After all, he looked just perfect to her. Their eyes met and he smiled at her. She smiled back, blushing like a school girl. *Oh, no he didn't just make me blush*, thought Mimi, trying to get a grip on herself.

The rest of the band began to improvise with Jovanni's worship and together the song began to symphonize. Mall goers began to mill around the stage and gaze at the band members as they transformed into psalmists for the King of kings. Jovanni ministered to the mass in song, and the words he sang were his testimony, unabridged and true.

Then Jovanni began to speak as the music played gently in the background.

"The Lord, he changed me, rearranged me. I never thought I knew, it was possible to do. I used to look around the world for a man to love me. I thought I knew who would be right for me. I thought I knew men were what I sought after, but the Lord took me out of a life that was not right for me and turned me around to His will for my life. He showed me that He made me a man. He took my hand and led me down a straight path. He transformed me into the man He made me to be. Now I seek only my Lord and Savior Jesus Christ. I'm changed, dedicated, to the Lord. I'm not ashamed to tell the world what God has done. He promised me He'd care for me. He promised me that He'd keep me. He's ordered my steps and I haven't slipped back into that worldly life. God has changed me."

Oh, my, thought Mimi, as she began to catch on to Jovanni's words. *He is—or was—gay! Is that what he's been changed from? Come on, that's not even possible, or is it?* Mimi was challenged by the thought, but wondered about the consequences of longing for someone who was on the "other side." Was he really *delivered*?

Try me, she heard a voice whisper deeply within her.

You're on, she thought. And she decided right then and there that if God could transform a homosexual, mend her sister's broken heart, maybe this God, this Jesus, was more than she could ever imagine or dream He could be. *That's deep,* she thought. Tears were streaming down Mimi's face as she prayed silently from her heart to the Lord. *Thank you Jesus for showing me that you're all I truly need. What can I do so you can change me into what you want me to be? Please show me, Lord. Please change me. I know I've been out of Your will. I've sinned with men. Always looking for Mr. Right—and it was You all along, always there, calling me. Well today I'm answering, Lord. Deliver me from my past. I'm sorry for all I've done wrong. I want to change. Please, be my Lord and Savior. Please change me. I want to be dedicated to You, Jesus.* Before she knew it, she was on her knees, and so many people around her were crying out the name of Jesus, begging to be changed. God was moving at the mall, changing hearts, changing minds, changing victims into victors and seekers into finders. What a wonderful change.

AFTER THE ALTER CALL many people were running to the stage to give their lives to the Lord. Mimi was one of seventy-five converts that night who were delivered by Jesus, who through one keyboardist, brought forth a message of repentance and deliverance from a sinful life.

Later that evening after many of the people had disbursed, Mimi approached Jovanni and poured out her heart to him.

"I was so confused when I came here tonight. I confess, I was looking you up and down. But your song made me realize that's not why I came here tonight. I'm sorry that I was sizing you up, I mean, I thought you were a player and I'm not talking keyboard player," said Mimi, smiling.

Jovanni looked deeply into Mimi's eyes and asked her, "Has Jesus delivered you tonight?"

"Yes, I feel like I've been washed and filled. I feel light. I feel free like a new me has been unleashed."

"That's how I feel too, Mimi. I feel that way every time I worship Him. It's not just a one-time feeling you get when you 'get saved' suddenly. Jesus continues to fill my cup every day. When I wake up in the morning, I arise and minister to the Lord in song. He ministers right back to me with His loving touch of grace and mercy. I really can't explain it. I just love Him."

Jovanni and Mimi began to walk together after he packed up his keyboard. He escorted her to the parking lot where her SUV was parked.

"It was nice meeting you, Mimi. I hope to see you Sunday, or maybe sooner," Jovanni said inquisitively.

A little nervous and unsure, Mimi offered her telephone number to him, wondering if he would be interested in calling her.

"Call me sometimes, Jovanni—I liked talking with you tonight. Call me, okay?"

He smiled and promised he would call. She watched him as he walked away, hoping he would call her that night. After he'd reached his navy blue pickup truck, although he could not hear her, she whispered softly, "Good night, Jovanni." He turned around as though he felt her words, and he smiled at her once more and waved goodbye.

CONSUMING FIRE

"For I, saith the LORD, will be unto her a wall of fire round about, and will be the glory in the midst of her... Sing and rejoice, O daughter of Zion: for, lo, I come, and I will dwell in the midst of thee, saith the LORD."
— Zechariah 2:5, 10 (KJV)

When you give your heart to the Lord, He rejoices over you with love and occupies you with great passion. His love is a consuming fire. He promises to become your personal Firewall. He protects you. He takes you from glory to glory as you become rooted in Him and devoted to Him.

As we walk daily with the Lord, a love song resonates in our spirit. We know He's there, living inside of us, and transforming us each day. He is a flaming fire in the midst of us and our souls are set on fire for Him. We desire to please Him with our very breath and are no longer so concerned about pleasing ourselves. He is the fire within us that makes us go on. He is our passion. He is first in our lives. He is our Heavenly Bridegroom, our First Love.

Chapter 7

Light My Fire

MIMI WAS ON FIRE FOR CHRIST every since that Friday night at The Plaza. She felt like all her wrongs were erased and a new birth was occurring inside her heart. She wanted to tell everyone about her new Lover, starting with Shenir.

"I had a really nice time on Friday night," Mimi began as she rode with Shenir in her new luxury car to pick up Zionna from preschool.

"Well, it's written all over your face, Mimi. You're in love aren't you?"

"Yes, I am!"

"Jovanni is a nice guy. He's been through a lot—not someone to play games with," said Shenir. "I hope you're for real—he's my brother in Christ, you know."

"Shenir, I don't think you understand."

"Oh, I understand completely," Shenir said sharply. "I saw you two walking together after the service. Don't you think I know you, Mimi? You're moving fast in for the kill, Ms. Thing. It's like, that's all you ever do when you go out—hunt for a man. I'm just sick of it, Mimi!"

"Wait a minute Sister Shenir! Okay. Thank you for letting me know what's on your mind, but guess what—the man I'm in love with is not Jovanni. I admit, I was checking him out, and maybe it would be nice if he called and we could start getting to know each other. But let me tell you who I really love—JESUS!"

"Mimi, you really shouldn't use the Lord's name in vain like that I mean—what—"

"Shenir, I'm not using His Name in vain, I mean I am in love with Jesus," Mimi clarified. "Would you stop judging me. I mean, I know my past has been wild, but believe me when I say this: I have fallen in love with Him."

Shenir was quiet for a moment, as she studied Mimi's freckled face. Then she burst out in joyful laughter.

"Oh, my Lord! Mimi, I'm so happy. Girl, I didn't mean to say all those things. That is wonderful! You finally gave your heart to Mr. Right! Hallelujah! I've been praying for you to come around, girlfriend!"

Mimi, blushed. A rush of excitement went through her entire body as she began to tell her sister how her life and her heart had been changed.

"I know, Mimi, it's like a new lease on life. Jesus lifts you up in your spirit and keeps you on a spiritual high."

"Shenir, I can't stop talking about Jesus. I can't stop thinking about Jesus. When I got home on Friday, I blew the dust off of my Bible that Mamasita gave me when I graduated from eighth grade. I couldn't even put it down. I read the book of Matthew, Mark, Luke and John, and didn't stop reading until dawn."

"Mimi, you can't stop there. You've got to join church and get into some classes to help guide you. He has lit your fire. Keep it lit and let the fire grow with worship, prayer, service and study."

"That's what I want to do, Shenir. He's all I want."

"Praise the Lord!"

THANKSGIVING DAY WAS A LITTLE DIFFERENT this year for Shenir. With Shane gone, she convinced her family to try something untraditional with her. Mimi, Shenir, Mamasita and little Zionna broke bread with the Showbread Saints, a ministry in her church dedicated to serving food to the less fortunate at a local homeless shelter. There was plenty of food to go around more than once. Shenir brought her famous macaroni and cheese, Mamasita made two turkeys and Mimi made a huge pot of string beans and potatoes. Zionna helped pass out pre-wrapped plates to the visitors.

"Here you go sir," said Zionna as she gave a heavy plate of food to a bearded man with sparkling doe-like brown eyes. He smiled and took his seat after thanking her.

"Mamasita, will you pass me the apple dumplings," said Shenir, as she put the finishing touches on the desert table. "Mimi, I could sure use a hand."

"Girl, just a moment," Mimi was polishing off a spoonful of dressing, dropped the spoon into the dishwater in the kitchen sink and tied her apron back on. She rushed to her sister's side to help serve dessert plates to the guests.

The bearded man approached the sisters. "You all are so kind. May my Father in Heaven bless you both." He smiled and walked away. Mimi and Shenir and Mamasita looked at each other and smiled. Mamasita stepped up and hugged both her daughters and said, "I think we just served an Angel of the Lord."

SOMETHING ABOUT THE NAME JESUS was being sung by the choir and the praise team as Mimi entered the Shekinah Glory Christian Center flanked by Shenir and little Zionna that Sunday after Thanksgiving. Worship dancers were waving banners and shaking tambourines as they twirled in a spiritual ballet unto the Lord. The congregation was on their feet in unison giving God praise, waiving their hands. Mimi was overcome with a new found love for

Jesus as she too was swept away by the love song of Jehovah Elohim.

Shenir too was caught up in Christ. Her life was now dedicated to His service. She reserved her heart for His Highness. Shenir had made up her mind to completely live for Jesus. She trusted Him with her life. It was a time of great refreshing for both her and her sister Mimi.

Shenir felt joy and peace as she watched her brothers and sisters in Christ throughout the sanctuary worshipping the Lord. Shenir laughed silently to herself as she thought about how two sisters who were so different fell in love with the same One who gave His life for them. Shenir was a servant who worked day after day to please Jesus, and Mimi had discovered her True Love. Mimi was immersed in worship as she laid out in the isle on the floor. *We're a modern day Mary and Martha, each with our own expression of love for Jesus,* she thought. Shenir prayed, "Thank you, Lord, for bringing us close to you."

LATER THAT SUNDAY EVENING SHENIR went to the YMCA to hear Dirksen preach. She had begun seeing more of her old friend over the past few weeks since Shane's death. He called to check on her and stopped by periodically to see if she needed anything. He kept inviting her to return to his ministry at the YMCA, but she hadn't been back since that moving service he led in September. So, she decided to accept his invitation this evening.

As Dirksen spotted Shenir, he motioned from his seat for her to come and sit with him. He smiled at her as she arrived and sat beside him.

"I'm so glad you're here. I prepared a special sermon. I know you will love it."

"Dirksen, if it pleases God, that's all that matters."

He grinned from ear to ear and got up to give his sermon. He began.

"Go with me to John, Chapter 14, Verse 18, and let us read:

'I will not leave you comfortless. I will come to you.'

"Jesus made this promise to His disciples. He had just broken bread and given wine at the Last Supper, and Judas had just left to betray Him. There He was seated with the remaining disciples revealing to them that He was going away. At that moment, He assured them of His presence and His return and their personal comfort.

"Jesus was about to lay down His life and be crucified on a cross so that we would be forgiven for our sins, and He was concerned about our comfort.

"In John, Chapter 14, Verse 2, Jesus said, '...I go to prepare a place for you.' So not only is He concerned about our comfort, He also wants to make sure that we eternally have a roof over our heads.

"Our Lord cares for us like a Bridegroom for His Bride. We belong to Him and He takes our needs very seriously. That's why in the next verse, He promises that once the place is ready, He's going to come for us. The question is, Are you ready or not?"

The church stood to their feet, many shouted, "Yes."

Dirksen continued, "In Revelation Chapter 3, Verse 20, the Lord Jesus tells us '...I stand at the door and knock.' Well, I've got news for everyone: He's here! So I ask you again, are you ready or not?" Dirksen clapped his hands.

Many more attendees were yelling, "Ready!"

"Somebody ought to let Jesus in today! He's been knocking at the door of your heart way too long. Now, He's ready to come in and have dinner with you, but you've been too busy, or you've been too worldly, or you've been doing your own thing, or you've been getting your groove on, or you've been too lost and turned out! Can I get a witness somebody?"

Everyone in the gym was shouting. Shenir cried out, "Hallelujah!"

"If you're ready to receive Jesus Christ, the Son of God, as your Lord and Savior today, pray this prayer with me now with all your heart unto the Lord:

"Lord Jesus, I repent of my sins. I believe You are the Son of God and that You died on the cross for my sins. I believe You were raised by the hand of God the Father on the third day. I accept Your gift of salvation, and I receive you as my Lord and Savior. I receive You into my heart. Amen!"

People throughout the gym were giving their hearts to Jesus. Shenir had tears in her eyes for she was so moved by the power of God flowing through Dirksen.

Dirksen looked to Shenir for her approval, and she smiled and knodded her positive response back at him. He smiled at her. Secretly, he desired to see her again. For the one thing he longed for but still had not found was his Mrs. Right, but he was patient in his belief that the Lord would lead him to her. *Could it be Shenir?* he hoped.

As Shenir watched Dirksen blessing the new believers, she knew in her heart at that moment the answer to the question that the still small voice inside of her proposed the last time she heard Dirksen preach. This time, she answered Him—*yes, he is the one*. That was when Shenir began to see Dirksen in a whole new light and somehow knew he had always been meant for her. They shared a common interest, their love for Jesus. Then she thought, *The Lord works in mysterious ways.*